AUSSIE
PRISON
BREAKS

Published by Brolga Publishing Pty Ltd
ABN 46 063 962 443
PO Box 12544
A'Beckett St
Melbourne, VIC, 8006
Australia
email: markzocchi@brolgapublishing.com.au

National Library of Australia Cataloguing-in-Publication entry

      Tog, Joe.
      Aussie Prison breaks: not all escapees are desperados
      9781922036476 (pbk.)
      Criminals--Australia--Biography.
      Escapes--Australia.

      364.30994

Printed in China
Cover design by David Khan
Typeset and design by Imogen Stubbs

AUSSIE PRISON BREAKS

NOT ALL ESCAPEES ARE DESPERADOS

JOE TOG

DEDICATED TO DAWN (H G O)

A true and loyal friend who stuck with me through the bad times.

THE AUTHOR

Isolated in a small cage at Brisbane's maximum-security prison, awaiting trial, the author composed a series of short narratives for his defence-barrister. The purpose was to overcome confusion with the chronology of events leading up to his arrest in far North Queensland. That barrister (now a Queensland Court Judge) commented to his client during the trial, that the notes gave him a clarity that he did not normally get from cold facts and dates. Out of that comment grew this story.

THE STORY

Interrogation and incarceration; escape from two prisons; on-the-run travel: just some of the events that occur as you journey with the writer. It is a true chronicle and does not unfold as one might expect. It's sad in some places, funny in others, but at all times a lesson in life.

I wonder?

Would you understand,

If I just took my heart

And placed it—in your hand!

CONTENTS

MAXIMUM SECURITY

HE WHO IS THE ENEMY OF

MY ENEMY——IS MY FRIEND

ARAB PROVERB

SATURDAY 28TH JUNE 1980
ADELAIDE, SOUTH AUSTRALIA

The night was cold and overcast. Rain-clouds blocked the moon and stars. In the shadow of a high redbrick wall a big man crouched, unshouldering a rucksack, while studying a three-storey building nearby. A small man in grey coveralls knelt by him.

The building stood in an aitch (H) design, topped with steep metal roofs. Each floor had rows of small apertures, dark and multi-barred. Bright arc lights lit the entire area and a gloomy quiet reigned.

There was a gust of wind and the two men, the rucksack swaying between them, ran awkwardly across the open quad and into the shadow of the building's rear. They quickly assembled a short ladder; then climbed onto a recessed roof that covered a section of the ground floor—a kind of cul-de-sac—in between the arms of the building.

Drops of rain spattered the silent intruders as they carefully edged their way towards the central arm of the Yatala prison's maximum security block: B-Division. The time: 2:30am.

✛ ✛ ✛

Heart pounding, I awoke frightened, alone in the dimly lit cell. I stared at the flickering shadows on the walls, knowing that it was not a nightmare that gripped my mind. It was something else: a whirring, flapping sound that broke the still of the night as it filtered to me through the barred aperture high above my head.

THE BLANKET ROSE EERILY OFF THE BED, RISING TO THE WINDOW ABOVE...

I thought... pigeons? Yes, that's what it was! The roosting birds had been disturbed and were flying about, in and out of the light. I sat up to think about the phenomena and, as I did, a 'thing' came clattering in through the bars!

Shocked, I instinctively flung the blanket over it as it landed near my feet—scrambling up the wall at the head of the bed to get away from whatever it was. The blanket rose eerily off the bed, rising to the window above, to stop with a thud against one of the inner bars. On the nape of my neck, the hairs stood on end.

I leapt out from under the dangling shroud and off the bed, gasping for breath, fearful of what it might be. No bird could have done that! My mind raced on—yet if not, what then? I was on the third floor!

Without thought, I had grabbed the cell's small stool for defence against whatever had snatched my blanket and scared the wits out of me: every sense and nerve-end was trembling on edge. But as I stared at the blanket I saw that something shiny gripped it to the bar with a steady force. And recognition bloomed. What I saw was a small grapple-hook!

A flood of thought swamped my mind while I stood rooted, trying to make sense out of what was happening. I slowly lowered the stool. Could it be the police—impossible! Maybe friends? Or an enemy!

Yes, that's who it had to be! But… why this way? Jumping on to the bed again, my paranoia in full flight, I stood propped in the corner under the window-sill, with the stool raised as a shield, waiting…

A sudden stream of light, beamed from above me, lit the cell's floor near the door. I swallowed. My mouth was bone-dry. A voice, called into the cell: "Joe! Joe Tog, you there?" I didn't make a sound.

The torch-beam touched the bed's foot, crossed the cell to the small cupboard, then paused. The tension grew too much for my legs. I changed position.

The creak of the bed had hardly begun before the beam of light was back, questing at the foot of the bed, unable to reach me. Louder now and angry, the European voice said, "We here to get you out, Joe—not hurt you. Block up the door!" He was right of course. If his intention were to harm me, he would already have done it with a minimum of fuss.

▲ Yatala prison

Though still frightened, I stepped off the bed into the light and walked to the door before peering back. All I saw was the vague shape of the blanket as it dropped. I blanched, but nothing happened except that the torch went out.

From within the dark cell, I could see that some kind of screen had been fitted, which blocked out most of the incoming light. The intruder ordered, "Get water ready; and block the door!" Then I smelt acetylene. With a pop and a flash the cell filled with orange light and a loud hissing sound.

I wasn't equipped mentally to argue the point and even if I had been, I doubt that I would have gotten anywhere with him. Prison regime debilitates one's ability to make decisions and the man at the window was enough to daunt anyone. I doused water over my towel and sheets before packing them into the gaps of the door.

The cell quickly filled with acrid fumes and the sharp smell of burning metal. To avoid fire and smoke, I moved the bed and poured water over everything that the hot drops of metal spattered. The fear was leaving me. I had been without stimulation for so long that even this—the unknown—was beginning to excite me!

My thoughts tumbled over each other … how had he known my cell's position? Who was he? Why was he doing it? And especially, what was wanted of me? Better to cooperate now and argue about it later.

Could it be Fritz, my co-accused? Not at the window of course—but somewhere behind it, I concluded, hopeful, grasping at the thread of reason. Because, only six months prior, Fritz had disappeared from the prison early one morning and, to the chagrin of the prison staff, without anyone seeing him. Before going, he'd sworn that he would help me in some way.

A gate clanged shut below; the flame flickered out. "Is the door blocked up?" Came the demanding question.

"Yes," I replied. "It's the best I can do," knowing as he did, that the gate indicated a prison warder was conducting an internal check of the cell block, section by section. Three to each floor and mine would be the last.

I fanned a towel, hoping to disperse the smoke, but not realistically expecting success. It would soon be discovered, I thought. Some of it must have seeped out into the passageway.

Apparently the man at the bars thought the same. He urged, "Wet the packing and shove in more!" The cutting torch was re-lit.

I unravelled toilet paper and did as he ordered. I presumed he knew what he was doing—I'd never have had the balls to continue!

Another gate clanged. The flame now gnawed away at the inner bars.

In my minds-eye, I watched the screw climb the stairwell to the middle landing and then, after an eternity of waiting, another gate slammed shut. Soon it would be the top landing. Mesmerised, I awaited the inevitable.

But it never came. For a reason unknown to me then, the screw didn't enter the third level. I waited for it while the cutting continued... and waited... until my bladder clamoured to be emptied. Only then did I realise that I stood almost naked!

Grabbing a jumper and shorts, I quickly dressed and when pulling my socks on, the flame sputtered out. The cell was black as coal as I groped about. "Take these bars," came the order. "And they hot." I jumped up on the locker as the cover came off the window, venting the cell; and light flooded in.

The first bar I grabbed burnt my hands, but I hung on until I got it to the floor. I dunked a singlet in water for the next one, and then the next: four in all.

My pulse went erratic when I heard him say, "Come out head first," and my heart hurt for a few beats. I tried to say something, but whether it was protest or agreement did not matter; my mouth was a glue-pot. I obeyed.

I climbed back onto the locker and pulled myself up to the aperture—but the smallness of the hole defeated me. I had to get back down.

With the stool on top of the locker, I was able to put my head and shoulders into the cavity. I wriggled and pulled my way into the tunnel-like hole. The hot stubs of the removed vertical bars scraped my chest.

On the outside wall, four of the horizontal bars had been cut almost through and bent aside. A nylon rope hung from the bars down to a tin roof two floors below, where two men were hunched over a rucksack tying it closed.

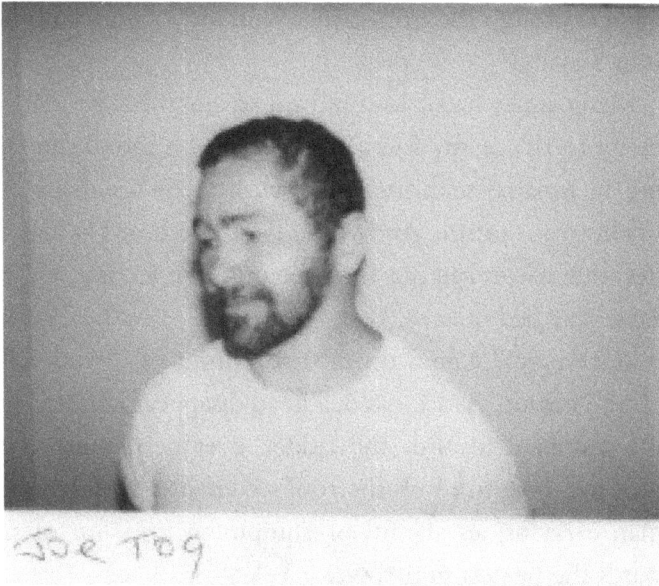

Joe T09

Gradually, I wormed my way out, drizzly rain cooling me, until my groin scraped on the rough stubs of metal. I took hold of the wet rope and put a twist of it round my wrist before proceeding further.

Muscles straining, I gingerly turned myself over as the rest of my legs slid out, to drop down and hang with my back against the wall. The descent to the roof was quick and easy.

When I touched the tin and let go of the rope, I trod on a nail head and my foot pained—I'd forgotten footwear! But I wasn't given time to muse on it. Both men had already crabbed their way in the guttering along the wall to the outer end of the cell block. I hurried after them, frightened of being left behind, not yet comprehending the magnitude of what was occurring.

I was surprised and gratified when, at my feet, I heard, "Good luck, Joe! You deserve to win." A cigarette-end glowed in the dark. Crouching down, I spoke a few words of cheer through the iron-grilled window of a ground floor cell in S-wing.

Many times had I lowered on string, messages and bits of news to Bruce, my friend, to keep up his morale and give those in isolated security a link with what was happening in mainstream prison. And while talking, I heard at least another four voices call out their regards. The feeling of camaraderie warmed me.

"Get here!" Came the hoarse command. "And follow with the ladder." As I looked, a head disappeared from sight.

I stumbled towards the ladder, over dead pigeons and bits of masonry, to reach the roof's edge just in time to spot a man carrying an armful of equipment, run out of sight towards the nearest gun-tower.

The bright lights of the prison were blinding as I climbed down and shouldered the ladder, to race after them towards an open gate under the menacing tower. I didn't even feel the sharp gravel under my feet.

After passing through the gateway I halted, grounding the ladder, because the small man had waited to pull the damaged gate closed behind me. Reaching down he picked up a coil of oxygen and acetylene hosing, and leather straps, "Go through that gate and follow the wall to the fence," he told me pointing.

I did what he wanted, running with the ladder down two steps and through another forced-open gate, entering a dark section of the prison (or relatively so, compared to the section just left). At least now I didn't feel like a sitting duck! Yet I was amazed that it had gone this far, undetected by the surveillance-cameras and patrolling screws. Never for a moment did I expect, or hope, for success.

Ahead of me I saw the big man crawling under the prison's outer cyclone-wire fence. As I ran towards him he stood up and slung the heavy rucksack on his back with ease. He signalled me to follow, then turned and lumbered into the night.

Under the wire I went, on my back, only to hear the scary pound of rapidly approaching feet. My jumper snagged on the wire; but I wrenched it free, making the fence twang and rattle in my haste to face my fear.

The man who'd cut the bars and waited at the gate slithered under the fence and onto his feet with hardly a pause and, picking up the ladder, ran on past me saying, "Quickly! They're moving inside." I scrambled up and raced along behind him. The big man I never saw again that night.

Out of my depth emotionally and being controlled by my limbic centre, I fled down a steep track to a creek where I caught up with the man and took the ladder. We followed the watercourse; him leading and setting the pace, without a rest for at least a kilometre until we reached a bridge and road.

A staccato one-sided conversation ensued. All I could do was listen. My pulse fluttered and my lungs heaved. He pointed across the road at a side street where a vehicle with its parking lights on sat. "Things you need, in a bag," he said. "Leave the car at airport." He handed me two

UNDER THE WIRE I WENT, ON MY BACK, ONLY TO HEAR THE SCARY POUND OF RAPIDLY APROACH-ING FEET.

keys, then told me the address of a safe house.

During the telling, a dozen questions sprang to mind, but only one was spoken out loud: "Why did you get me out?" The need to know dominated.

He answered in one burst. "Another team... the cops after. They know you could have traded them... and got out. This way you −" and then something beeped in his pocket. "Go!" He urged me. "Go now!" And ran back towards the prison, out of sight.

I huddled up in the long grass, in shadow and falling rain, irresolute, not knowing what to do. These men (and others) risked their freedom for a principle, I thought, and it would be petty of me to lessen the gift by not making the most of it. Besides, police treachery had put me in prison. My only 'crime' had been failure to succumb to their threats and violence. A righteous anger grew.

Finally, mind made up, I crossed over and got in the car, to start the motor and drive away. And during those first few minutes of driving while searching for a dark place to park and dress, the reality of my escape was thrust upon me—a police car caught up, and swished by—like a knife-blade in the bowels.

A reaction set in. All the suppressed fear of my arrest and legal tribulations overwhelmed me. The thought of being in the clutches of the two detectives who'd set-me-up filled me with dread. I had to turn off into a side street and stop the car. The dash clock showed the time: 3:40am.

My past returned. I re-lived some of the incidents involving my arrest, and imprisonment.

ARREST 1

FRIDAY 8TH SEPTEMBER 1978
ADELAIDE, SOUTH AUSTRALIA

The barking of my kelpie pup, Sahm, is what woke me. I slid out of bed, leaving Diane undisturbed in her sleep, and stepped to the window of my caravan to investigate.

On the other side of the fence in the street, I saw bright headlights near the side-gate of the house I lived behind. When the lights of the vehicle doused, I could see that it belonged to an associate of mine, Fritz. I put on a coat and stepped out (telling my little friend to stop his yapping) to find out what Fritz wanted of me so early in the day.

He was quick to explain that when in Adelaide a fortnight earlier he had pre-arranged to have his camper van's electrical wiring re-done. He said he needed a place to leave his van's contents for the day, presuming that I'd not object. He had stayed overnight before.

"Sure, Fritz," I agreed, having learnt long ago that a straight yes or no, is best with him. "Stack it at the back of my 'van, or under it if you think it might rain."

"I do not think it will rain," he replied in his precise English, rambling on about the weather and his trip over from Sydney.

I pretended to listen, not interested at 4:00 am. And at the first gap in his travelogue, I ended it. "I'm going back to bed. It's obvious you don't need me to unload; or do you?"

"Joe, I am not tired. I appreciate your offer, but I myself will do it."

"When'll you be back to pick it up?"

"It will take four hours to wire my van," he answered, "and I do not -"

"Yeah, yeah," I cut him off. "I'll see you when I see you, okay?

We'll talk then." I stepped into the van and closed the door.

Diane asked, "Is that Fritz again?"

"Don't worry about it," I assured her, climbing into bed. Knowing she disliked him, I explained what was happening to avoid further questions.

"He's leaving some stuff from his van, but he'll be back to pick it up this afternoon."

I really was tired and the last thing I wanted was to talk about Fritz. Despite the slight noise of things outside, I fell easily back into sleep.

+ + +

The sun was up before me. I went to greet Fritz but his camper van was gone. In a neat stack at the caravan's rear stood a pile of boxes and goods, covered part over with a small tarpaulin and guarded by Sahm. Grabbing a towel and toiletries from the van, I entered the house by the back door.

After a refreshing shower, I returned to Diane. She watched me dress from the warmth of her bed, snuggled in under the blanket. I was about to spoil her sleep-in

▲ Fritz

and she knew it. But I enjoyed watching her psyche up. She *really* hated the chilly mornings of Adelaide.

"Well, come on. Get up!" I urged. "If we're going shopping today you'd better pull your finger out!"

Grimacing at my rudeness, Diane leapt out and pulled on her dressing gown. In one motion she grabbed a towel and fled the warm van. As usual she forgot to take her slippers.

A knock at the door caused me to turn in the middle of dressing and find Natalie, a precocious eleven-year-old from the house, standing there with her two younger sisters. "Do you want us to wash your car today, Uncle Joe? We'll do it for just three dollars!" They watched me expectantly.

I pretended to give it heavy thought. The girls would

have to be the worst car-wash team in S.A.—but the elbow grease they always put into it was worth the money.

I finally said, "Alright," and watched three smiles appear. "Only this time I want the inside cleaned—a perfect job—not a cent if it's not perfect! Fair enough?"

There were nods and shouts and never for a moment did they doubt that theirs would not be a perfect detailing. They ran off with my keys, shouting excitedly to each other, to get what was needed for cleaning the car. I picked up Diane's slippers and followed them into the house.

"Is that you, Joe?" Called Diane from the bathroom when she heard me greeting the kids' parents in the kitchen.

"Yeah, Di. What do you want?" I asked knowing full well what she wanted.

"My slippers; will you get them for me?" She wheedled. "Please?"

I said, "No! You left them," and quietly put them against the door.

"Oh! Please get them…"

+ + +

Breakfast over, Diane and I went out to see how the girls were going with my car. But when we got there *I could not believe* the chaos I saw on the street. Every single thing (and I mean *everything*)

EVERY SINGLE THING THAT COULD BE REMOVED FROM THE PONTIAC HAD BEEN AND THEN STREWN IN DISARRAY ALONG THE FOOTPATH!

that could be removed from the Pontiac had been and then strewn in disarray along the footpath! Even the spare wheel from the gaping boot (a monster which even I had difficulty lifting) lay in the gutter. There were mats, clothes, buckets and water, actually making me angry! It felt a bit like being stripped naked in public. But as I took in their earnest, grimy faces, so determined to detail that bronze beast of mine, I relented.

Diane helped the little ones while Nat and I turned the path's disorder into a neater line against the fence. Then, while Di and her two hinderers put the inside of the car back together, Natalie and I arranged the car's boot: wheel, tool-box, car-jack and spade, a barbecue-set and axe, and last of all, a point 22 rifle wrapped in a hunting jacket. Eventually the footpath appeared normal again.

The girls each collected a dollar and before they had left for the local shop to spend their 'hard earned' cash, Diane and I bid everyone goodbye and headed for the shopping centre at Elizabeth, a northern suburb.

+ + +

I had just pulled in behind the shopping complex when another car stopped nearby. Two men, casually attired, got out and looked our way. I took little notice of them (thinking they were admiring my car) until one strode towards my car. The other one went behind the Pontiac and out of sight.

My senses went on Red Alert—a possible robbery! I hastily leaned over Diane and locked her door, then locked mine as the man tried to open it. The window was half open.

I said to him, "What do you think you're doing?"

"Don't worry about that!" He snapped. "Get out of the vehicle, now!"

"Fuck off!" I snarled. "Who do you think you are?"

"I'm a police officer, a member of the drug squad."

"Prove it!" I demanded. No way was I moving till I sighted some I.D. He flashed me his identification card and search warrant: he was a Jack, all right. I opened the door and told Diane to do the same.

Outside on the asphalt he told me that he intended to search my car for drugs. I was indignant and had some very biting comments to make about drug-users while he rummaged in the glove box, under the seats and behind the dashboard. Finally, having found nothing, he demanded that the car's boot be unlocked and opened.

By this time the other detective was questioning Diane and had moved to the police car with her. His shabby manner held my attention until the one ferreting about in the boot asked, "Who owns the point two-two?"

Without thinking, I answered, "My friend, Diane." But in reality I owned the rifle, though it was unregistered.

"Do you own this rifle, Diane?" He called out to her, holding it aloft.

Diane looked at me as I nodded. She then replied, "Yes, I do."

"Do you have it registered in your name?"

And when Diane answered, "No I don't," the detective called out, "Put her in the vehicle." I was incensed, angered enough to punch this jerk! But keeping it cool, I called to Diane, "Don't worry, love! I'll have you out straight away."

Another curt order. "Hand me your wallet." I gave it to

him without comment.

While pawing through its contents he observed, "There is a large sum of money here! Where did you get it?"

"The bank of course!"

"Can you prove that?"

"Certainly!"

"Prove it to me."

"What? Right now?"

"Yes! Otherwise I'm going to arrest you for being in possession of money suspected of being unlawfully obtained," he coldly stated.

"Most of those fifties run in consecutive order" I exclaimed. "Think about it! They HAD to come from a bank." (And they did, in Salisbury, two days before.)

"Are you able to prove that to me now?"

"Not today, no. But on Monday I certainly can; after the weekend."

"Then I'm placing you under arrest." He quickly handcuffed me and said, "Get into the police vehicle," taking me by the arm and pushing me.

"Lock-up my car first!" I demanded. "I'm not moving anywhere till it is." I fumed with anger, frustrated by his arrogant manner.

He grabbed the keys from the ignition, locked my car and kept the keys. I climbed into the police car's rear next to Diane. The car drove away from mine as I spoke in a whisper to Diane.

The passenger detective turned and told us not to talk. Ignoring him, I continued to comfort Diane. He interrupted me and began questioning Diane about the rifle. I told her not to answer him without a solicitor being present to advise her. That was her legal right, I said.

He abused me—so I abused him! It quickly deteriorated into a slanging match of which I emerged the victor. By now my blood was well and truly up!

Full of rage, I told Diane, "Not one word to these pigs! Not one fucking word! Do you understand me, Diane?" She was on the edge of tears, so only nodded. The whole incident had blown her out.

"NOT ONE WORD TO THESE PIGS! NOT ONE FUCKING WORD! DO YOU UNDERSTAND ME, DIANE?"

I had nothing to fear. The worst I expected was to be hassled verbally, to have a few punches thrown at the local cop-shop, but nothing more serious than that. How wrong I was.

+ + +

Inside the police station, uniformed police led Diane away while I was taken upstairs and left sitting in a chair, still handcuffed, in a large duty room. A Constable sat there to watch me while they went away.

When they returned and the Constable had left, they searched me thoroughly. One thousand dollars was taken out of my back pocket and together with my wallet's content totalled $2,500. They interrogated me about the money.

Our conversation quickly grew heated, with me requesting access to a telephone and them demanding answers. Thwarted, I refused to continue dialogue with them until a solicitor was present to advise me. I sat mute - stubborn as a miner's mule!

Eventually they gave it up. Calling in the Constable standing outside the room, they left me. And during the next hour the Constable, quite friendly really, tried to start a conversation. I treated him to silence—Diane was on my mind. They were obviously interrogating her.

Twice, the narcs returned to show me articles they had taken out of my car. First a baseball bat from under the seat, then my pullout cassette player. They were obvious attempts to initiate conversation by accusation. But once committed to a role of silence, I intended to follow it through out of pure bastardry!

+ + +

Another constable replaced the first one as the day wore on. He tried similar conversational gambits with even less success. By now I refused to even acknowledge that I understood English.

The entire station's staff must have come up in two's and three's to gig at me, making snide comments on my parentage and ancestry. For all I know, they may have had bets on to see who could goad me into speaking. A change of shift came on duty.

The refrains started up then, with the baiting and insults:

"Sam's on his way here."

"You'll talk for Sam!"

"Wait 'til Sam gets you."

"They all confess to Sam!"

A nag of concern gradually shrouded my thinking. Sam was undoubtedly a Special Squad detective. And they are the same in every state: a mean lot, who start where the others stop.

I reviewed what might be coming: money suspected of being stolen or unlawfully gained; an offensive weapon (the base-ball bat); refusal to give them my name and address; plus owning an unregistered point-22. Petty stuff! Papers in the Pontiac's glove box and wallet would tell them whatever they needed to know about me. I was just being obstructive.

Very soon a flurry of activity below me sharpened my senses and before long the tread of heavy feet ascended the steps. I felt scared. The unknown always frightens. The door swung open and the Constable sprang to his feet.

A short, bearded, fat man stood filling the doorway. He ordered the Constable, "Get out of here," as he advanced into the room. A thin man tailed in behind him while four other detectives stayed at the door.

The fat man pugnaciously stated, "I'm Sam! You'll talk and talk until I decide you've spilled enough! Got that?"

I almost laughed in nervous release. I'd awaited a Mountain Man and instead Elmer Fudd had arrived. But wisely, I kept poker-faced. I'm not that naive—the awe in which he was held testified to hidden ability.

Fatso struck me on the cheek. "Talk! What's your name?" I stared past him at the crowded doorway. Had any other approach been used I may have broken my silence (worry erodes resolve), but threats and violence only strengthen me.

He grabbed my shackled wrists and towed me out of the room down the stairs and into a yard caged in steel, to shove me into a cell at the end. The door slammed closed, leaving me in lonely darkness as the night closed in.

+ + +

Early next morning, many long hours later, the gate to the cell block crashed open. I sprang off the bench pulse pounding. They were coming for me and their psychology was working. The door swung out with a clatter of keys.

Fatso and Skinny stood next to the uniformed jailer and behind them were another two detectives. They hustled me out of the yard and into the Police station.

Fatso advised, "We know who you are and all about you. Give us what we're after and you *might* get off lightly—or you'll wish you never came to this fucking state!"

At the top of the stairwell they steered me into a room barely able to contain the two desks and row of metal lockers filling it. Skinny pushed me down onto a chair between the desks against the east wall, while the two support detectives went past me to stand in front of the south window. On the other side of the first desk just inside the door, Skinny sat in front of a big typewriter, facing me. Fatso closed the door and stood glaring at me, his back to the lockers lining the west wall.

While Skinny performed the ritual of rolling paper and carbon under the platen, Fatso had lots to say about what crimes I had been involved in—according to him!

Skinny started to type. This surprised me. I definitely did not intend to take part in a Record of Interview, yet that's what it had every appearance of being. But I sat there mute, until finally the clacking of the keys halted.

Skinny read aloud from the curled sheet of paper. "I am detective… you are in police custody. Yesterday at noon, two members of the… and you have been cautioned of your rights. What is your full name?"

The fact that he then read out my real name without my having voiced it—unbeknownst to them, I'd changed it by deed poll and no longer used it—did not surprise me. The car had been purchased before the change. It was the next question that caught me by the throat.

"Three breaking offences… two safes cut open… and I further caution you." He stared at me. "What can you tell me about those offences?" My adrenalin rushed—no, gushed! They were accusing me of major crimes, not money and a baseball bat! I almost blurted out my indignation; but a sixth-sense stayed my breath and held me mute.

When Fatso spoke, he confirmed my worst fear: "If you don't tell us who did them, or give us names of who you think might have—and they have to be Victorians—then you get to wear the lot!" And he meant it.

Now I had every reason to remain silent. They were after a scapegoat and anything I said would only help them pull the noose tighter on my already exposed neck. Tension filled the room like smoke.

Skinny started typing again - typing down what Fatso had to say next. "I will help you all I can. Yes, I busted into those places."

I leapt up; bursting with indignation, but Fatso was ready for me. He shoved me back onto the seat, smiling at my dilemma. What he had said was supposed to have been my answer! No wonder he *always* got a confession! They were verballing me. I didn't know what to do next.

Slumped in the chair, I watched Skinny resume typing and Fatso relax back onto the metal lockers before I made up my mind to act. I hissed at Skinny, "You scumbag!" And spat at him across the desk. He jerked his seat back, mouthing oaths—I sprang to my feet reaching for the typewriter.

My sudden rush of activity caught Fatso flat-footed. He didn't make it to me. The heavy typewriter hit him square on the chest and while he fought with it, I headed for the door. I didn't get out though. They worked me over good; the other two kept completely out of it.

THE HEAVY TYPEWRITER HIT HIM SQUARE ON THE CHEST AND WHILE HE FOUGHT WITH IT, I HEADED FOR THE DOOR.

Luckily the commotion of the lockers being banged, and their language, soon attracted a senior officer. "What's going on here?" He demanded to know as soon as he stepped into the fray.

"He attempted to escape, sir!" Fatso blurted out to cover himself.

"We had to restrain him!" Put in Skinny, corroborating Fatso's lie.

The Inspector asked, "Were you actually trying to escape?" He sounded genuinely sceptical, but I wasn't coming into it.

My answer was stoic silence, though it sorely tested me standing there in handcuffs.

"Lock him back in a cell," said the Inspector.

At the bottom of the stairs, flanking me with three other jacks, Fatso boasted, "Let's show Joe what he's up against if he doesn't cooperate, eh?" And instead of stepping into the cell block they shepherded me out to a small, enclosed car park. My Pontiac was the nearest vehicle. Its passenger door hung open, with the carpet and seat-covers strewn on the ground. Fatso lifted up the car's boot-lid to reveal its contents.

Shocked, I stared in, thoughts reeling filled with dread by what I saw: coveralls and combat boots, a cassette player (not mine) and worst of all, a mini-oxygen and acetylene outfit and tool kit. It all sat jumbled up in the boot.

Contemptuously, I hawked phlegm and spat it onto the fat verballers smirking face. His retaliation was lightning fast, resulting in the blackest black eye that I have ever had—but it was worth the pain.

I was then pushed and shoved back to the cell block. Still stunned by the punch, I heard Diane's anguished voice cry out, "He hit me, Joe! The one with the snake ring." Her tear-swollen face peered out at me through a trap in the cell near the gate.

While the handcuffs were being removed, before they pushed me into the cell, I saw that Fatso was the wearer of the ring. The door slammed shut and they walked away laughing, at ease with their deed.

+ + +

That same morning at 10 am, I stood formally charged in the Magistrate's Court and consequently remanded to Adelaide Gaol—bail refused—on the following prima-facia 'evidence': "The prisoner has attempted to escape from police custody," the court was told by you-know-who, "and comes from Melbourne." The Police-Prosecutor went on to say, "Stolen property, as well as tools and oxygen and acetylene equipment used in safe-breaking had been discovered."

And according to the charging officer (Fatso), "had made full admissions to the offences as charged!" (Yes, they completed the concoction after locking me away.)

Heeding the crime sheet and the various allegations, it would have required two gangs to commit the quantity of offences alleged. Yet this confession duly admitting to sundry crimes, which the police relied on, unsigned, omitted to name any other member of the Pub Gang I supposedly led! Except unfortunate Fritz, whose particulars were gleaned from the property he had left behind my caravan. And so on.

Apparently my little dog had bitten one of them, carrying out his canine duty: so out of spite he was kicked to death! With a black eye, split lips, bruises and sore balls, I languished in Limbo, incarcerated to await Trial-by-Jury.

▲ Aerial view of Adelaide Gaol

TRANSPORT

VOWS BEGIN WHEN HOPE DIES

LEONARDO DA VINCI

FRIDAY 24TH NOVEMBER 1978
ADELAIDE, SOUTH AUSTRALIA

The metal-capped hangman's tower in Adelaide Gaol caught my boredom. I studied its grim outline against the morning skyline, while all around me the steady pacing of men awaiting trial continued. The yard thrummed with noise.

A warder, fat with soft living, came to the gate and called my name.

"Yes," I answered, turning to face him, the tower forgotten. "What do you want?"

"Bring all of your property to the gate, and wait," he bluntly ordered.

"Where am I going?" I wondered what the move meant.

"You'll find out when you get there," he snapped. "Now

get your stuff and stand at the gate like you're told!"

"Okay." These screws saw themselves as the thin line between social order and chaos. I went to get my few possessions.

After leaving the yard, I was escorted to the gaol's clothing store to be dressed in my own clothes; then escorted to the main entrance and left to stand in the area between the two gates where an inward facing police van waited. I enquired of the warder in charge, "Where am I going to, sir?"

"If you need to know you'll be told," was his curt reply. "Now stand there and keep quiet and wait!" He glared at me as he said it.

So I stood there, waited and watched, till my frowning co-accused also arrived at the gates. He was told to stand beside me, and he did, putting his boxes down, his sharp eyes missing nothing.

Quietly, I asked him, "Fritz, do you have any idea what this might be about?"

His stilted response was, "I do not know, Joe. I will ask the gate officer." And he did too, in his unique way; getting an answer far more caustic than the one I got, leaving us as much in the dark as before. So we waited... until two uniformed policemen emerged from an inner sanctum of the gaol and walked towards the police van. One held two official-looking folders and the other one carried two property bags—used to hold valuables of an accused when first admitted into gaol—which they put in the cab.

Fritz belatedly observed, "Our mention-date is a month away. Why do they take with us our property bags?" It was really pointless asking me. Worry has *never* solved a problem.

So I stood there waiting until finally the two policemen

came over to us. And while one handcuffed me the other one did the same to Fritz—with Fritz asking at least a half dozen rapid-fire questions, only to be given an uncivil, "Shut up! Get into the van!" Which he did. I followed in behind and the door slammed shut, before being securely bolted.

The outer gate swung open and the van reversed out. Up to this point it had all seemed normal, so I wasn't unduly concerned—until I spotted an unmarked police car with two detectives (the two who put me in prison) pull in behind us to closely tail the van! I soon knew that our destination was not to be the Adelaide Courthouse. Both vehicles sped out of the city and up through the encircling hills along the main highway, heading east towards the Victorian border.

It was Fritz who came up with part of the correct answer. "This is the way to Bordertown. Our trial venue must be changed to there, Joe. Two of the 'busts' that we are charged with —"

"Impossible!" I burst out. "My counsellor's assured me that it'll be heard at the Adelaide Sittings. I've still got witnesses to be interviewed to confirm my alibi and—anyhow, no trial date's been agreed to yet!" And after that short outburst, our conversation deteriorated into smouldering silence. I fumed.

Being driven at such reckless speed, it didn't take long before Fritz was able to tell me that we were soon to enter the township of Keith, where two of the offences occurred. I sat up with interest.

We had almost passed through the small town when, unexpectedly, the van braked, to turn right and halt in front of the local police station. The driver and passenger got out and entered the station. The tail car sat behind us. And when the two returned with five of the Keith police, Fritz and I readied ourselves to climb out; but that was not to be. They just stared in at us like patrons at a zoo, spoke amongst themselves, and then went back inside. It's a very unpleasant sensation trapped and at the mercy of others, handcuffed, not knowing what the future might hold… expecting the worst.

ONE TURN THREW FRITZ OFF HIS SEAT, SPINNING HIM INTO THE WIRE-MESH COVERING A SIDE WINDOW,

The two uniforms returned and changed places, with the van driving off southwards at a rapid pace even more dangerously driven than before, if that was possible! In fact, one turn threw Fritz off his seat, spinning him into the wire-mesh covering a side window, and scratching his nose and cheek. That injury, oddly, had a fortunate sequel soon to unfold.

Fritz solved the puzzle of where we were headed. "I think this is the original highway to Mount Gambier, the south-east capital where criminal trials are held. A remand section exists in the prison there." He rambled on, explaining to me in more detail, while I fulminated against the move south.

I didn't even know the prison existed! It was all news to me. At the time, all I knew was that I should *not* have been going there—or at least I should have been notified long beforehand.

Most of the offences of which I stood accused (falsely I must again add) had occurred in the north-east of the state and therefore the proper court venue - outside the state's capital

- was at Bordertown, not at Mount Gambier in the state's south-east! Pondering those aspects, a tentacle of dread gradually snared my thoughts as the van raced south through Naracoorte.

The large picturesque city of Mount Gambier is 300 kilometres out from Adelaide. As the police vehicles threaded their way through the streets of hurrying people, I could not avoid thinking of how few of us ever truly comprehend how abstract our freedom really is, and how easy it is to lose. A man much wiser than I once stated: 'The price of freedom is eternal vigilance'*. Almost daily I reflect on how true that is—and how easily my freedom had been snatched from me!

The prison, I saw when we arrived at it's imposing wood and iron front-gate, was set in behind pine trees with a few stone-built cottages near to the prison's north-west perimeter wall. A high cyclone-wire fence enclosed a big vegetable garden to the south. The prison walls were built of Mount Gambier stone—rustically attractive yellow sandstone, soft when quarried, which slowly hardens with air exposure. It was early colonial in structure.

A warder in blue stood near the entrance and, when approached and spoken to by one of the uniforms, he directed him to a much smaller gate in the sidewall where a button was pressed. Minutes later, two warders came out and spoke with the two in blue. The van's door was unlocked and we were told to climb out. The detectives behind watched every move.

When escorted into the prison, it's 'atmosphere' felt comfortable. The few gaol-inmates I saw in that first, fleeting

*Quote by Thomas Jefferson.

impression appeared to be cheerful—yet I felt that dread's grip tightening. Fritz and I were left to wait outside the Superintendent's office, while the police, after retrieving their 'cuffs finished their official duties inside.

When they departed ten minutes later, I was called into a large uncluttered office and told to stand at attention in front of the Superintendent sitting behind his desk. To my right, a small array of electronic equipment was visible on top of a wooden cabinet including a few two-ways and a C.B. base-unit. There was another device that I couldn't immediately identify by its dials and knobs. The Super began by officiously informing me that I was detained there lawfully and would remain in his custody until a court decided otherwise.

I said, "I've been transferred to here without knowledge of why. Are you able to shed some light on it for me?"

He replied, "Prisoner, I knew nothing of it myself before your arrival. But the warrant is quite clear," and here he held up a document to read aloud; "To be held on remand… bail denied… to stand trial at the Mount Gambier Sittings on the twenty-seventh day of November." He put the paper aside to peruse his desktop calendar, adding, "In three days time, Monday."

I continued to explain that, to my knowledge, "My barrister has not been notified of the trial venue change; would the prison notify him on my behalf?"

His reply was a succinct, "No, we're not a messenger service," and before I could respond, the telephone rang.

During his conversation I heard the words "faulty alarm circuit," instantly understanding what the other device was: a multi-alarm monitor used to control discrete sectors of the prison. I therefore paid much more attention than I would normally have to the ensuing talk. Apparently, one of the prison's sectors kept going off without a known cause and had to be fixed. It was referred to by the Principal Warder as remand-yellow. I filed the clue away.

After the phone had been re-cradled and our conversation resumed, the initial niceties got quickly lost. The Warden blew his cool, and ordered me out of his office. I thought: wait till he meets the Kraut... compared to him I'm a mute!

After changing into prison garb I was led away to the remand section (unconvicted persons) and advised of a few prison rules to abide by, before being locked in. The remand yard measured 5 metres wide by 15 metres long and was roofed over with red steel beams covered with black wire mesh. The surface I stood on was bare cement. The yard's south side had three cell doors in it plus the iron grill-gate I entered by. The gate had a large circular mirror placed strategically above it through which the yard could be observed from the outside without entering. The north side at the west end of the yard revealed one cell, positioned opposite the entry gate. It was a modern addition to the prison's construction, destined to be my cell while I was held there. I walked over and looked inside at its fittings. A ceramic sink sat to the door's left, and to the right was a stainless-steel toilet bowl. Against the back wall stood a double bunk, each with a mattress and neatly folded blankets. A small metal locker on castor-wheels waited next to a tired old tubular-steel chair. Nothing else.

Back in the yard, I noticed that abut the east side of this cell stood what was obviously once the original prison chapel; a large building erected out of Mount Gambier stone. It had been converted into a recreational day room for the remand prisoners. Noticing that the ex-chapel's roof extended beyond the end of the yard, I entered the day room to suss it out.

The spacious room had similar dimensions to the yard, but with a ceiling three metres high. The only entrance into it was via the one in the south-west corner of the building, a metre east of the cell in which I was to endure some harrowing nights. Even at this early stage I believe I'd already started to subconsciously consider escape as a means of complaint (if I may call it that) or at least as a way to prevent further abuse and make my side of the story public.

In the day room there were three teenage prisoners. Two were playing snooker and a third, sitting at a table nearby, cheered them on; but when they became aware of my silent presence in the room they stopped playing and went quiet.

I know what they saw, it's happened before. I'm not a tall man but I am solidly built. My arms are tattooed and it's been said that I look mean; but really, I'm not. Their game resumed when I advanced inside to look the room over.

The three were obviously new to prison mores and unsure about themselves so, wanting to keep it that way, I ignored their smiles and tentative greetings to disconcert them.

The day room's eastern end had been walled off. I could see through the iron-barred windows of the room's south wall into the yard. All windows in the northern side were sealed with bricks. I strolled back out to rest in the sunshine, sketching a mental layout learnt so far while waiting for Fritz to arrive.

When he turned up he was vocal and irate, and not making much sense. His cell turned out to be one of the original ones on the south side of the yard, diagonally opposite my cell—as far from me as they could site him.

At 3:00 pm we were taken out of the yard for a shower. And at 4:00 pm our dinner was brought to us on trays. An hour later we were all locked away for the night.

If ever you are locked away for an offence of which you ARE guilty, then it IS bearable, because since childhood we have learnt to accept punishment for our wrongdoings. But, if ever you are so unfortunate to end up in prison for something you did not do, then you will learn like I did, that it is unbearable! 'Fortunately' for me I have wandered the high precipice of crime; so the gauntlet of police procedure, court rigmarole, and prison rigour, had prepared me for when I most needed it—as a scapegoat! My turbid mind stilled and when the cell light flicked out at 10:00 pm I made up the bottom bunk and climbed in.

After midnight, I slept till dawn.

▲ Mt Gambier prison front entrance.

▼ Mt Gambier prison cells and outside.

ESCAPE

**WE PROMISE ACCORDING TO OUR HOPES
AND PERFORM ACCORDING TO OUR FEARS**

FRANCOIS DUC DE LA ROCHEFOUCAULD

SATURDAY 25TH NOVEMBER 1978
MOUNT GAMBIER, S.A

At 6:30am the cells were unlocked and our breakfast handed to us in the yard. Fritz and I sat together in the early morning sun, apart from the other three, quietly conversing.

It soon unfolded that during Fritz's reception parade the day before, he was asked if it was me who had caused his bruised cheek and cut nose. Fritz explained how it had occurred, but it's in the nature of custodians to seek out problems that do not exist; and so a plan was formed. At first it was to benefit only Fritz; but then, as circumstances presented themselves, I took the bait—willingly. Chance favours the prepared mind.

Fritz wanted to escape. If I helped him to break out, he

promised in return to help me later establish my innocence. He freely admitted to me then, (and later to a court) that it was him and others—not me—who committed the crimes that he and I were accused of jointly committing. So, in no way did I blame him for my plight—Fatso and Skinny were responsible for that!

For Fritz to have any realistic chance of fleeing he had to be in the older section of the prison; to us the new remand section appeared too secure. The dodge we agreed to try-on was to pretend that we had fallen out with each other; that it was now physically unsafe for him to be kept at risk with me; he should be for his own safety, removed from the remand section. My security classification precluded any chance of me being moved.

I started off by loudly calling him a German swine, then a few less friendly terms which made the young guys nervous and caused the screws, as hoped, to look in. I even threw a body punch at him! All that day, we glared at each other like bears at bay.

At 3:00 pm we were again taken for showers, but when we returned, we found to our surprise, as well as everyone else's, that our cells had been thoroughly searched during our absence! Our dinners were handed out; then after an hour or so the screws again locked us away for the night. Alone in the cell, I made up my bed and before climbing into it, switched on the prison radio…

I STARTED OFF BY LOUDLY CALLING HIM A GERMAN SWINE

to lay back listening, remembering the day of my arrest. Eventually sleep blanketed my thoughts.

✚ ✚ ✚

Monday morning, Fritz and I were taken outside the prison for an appearance in court. The hearing was brief because no one came forth to defend us. The prosecutor wanted to proceed that day; but Fritz and I argued the unfairness of proceeding without our advocates. All kinds of disputes ensued, till finally the Judge testily stated: "This case is to go ahead. It will commence on Thursday, whether or not your counsellors are present. You have two days to arrange it." He rambled on about legal procedure and Jury-panel selection, but I turned off mentally, knowing that I had Buckley's in his courtroom… unless I could re-shuffle the deck. Convicted, I would rot in stir! Fritz voiced identical conclusions as mine. We were back in prison before lunch.

Law and Order is quite swift—Justice takes a lot longer.

✚ ✚ ✚

What happened next at the prison reveals the unpredictability of man: how the best-laid plans can go awry. Three turnkeys entered the yard and told Fritz to gather up all his possessions. Fritz was very quick to comply and for once didn't swarm them with a barrage of words. He came out with his arms loaded up, and fronted to the open grill-gate where the screws stood watching the yard.

The screw in charge asked Fritz, "Where are you going?" A stern tone in his voice.

Fritz replied, quite reasonably, "Outside, sir. You said I am being moved to another cell."

"You are," purred the screw with the beginning of a smile. "Over there," and pointed at my cell!

Was it a malicious act to place two 'hostile' men together in a locked cell? Or instead, was it that they saw through our ploy? Whatever the reason, Fritz walked in silence to his new cell (probably stunned) and deposited his things on the top bunk. That presumably spiteful act was another step towards an event beyond our expectations. In less than two hours would come the clue that would unlock the path to our freedom: but neither of us knew that then. We were going with the current, caught in a stream of events.

+ + +

After returning from my shower, while Fritz straightened up the mess left by the searchers, I heard someone walking on the steel mesh over the exercise yard. Curious, I strolled out to investigate. Two men above us were talking to a third man in a suit standing near the Superintendent's office. From their talk, I soon learned that they were testing the roof alarms. Intermittent beeping sounds came from the office while they did things, unobserved, on the roof of the day room.

+ + +

When our dinners arrived an hour later, they were still at it up there and it was obvious that they couldn't locate and fix the fault. It irked them.

Before our dinner utensils were collected and counted, I heard one call, "Cut the yellow circuit out and see if that'll isolate it."

Above me I heard a man move away… then return to say, "Try it now, boss."

And the circuit was tested by the man on the ground, who called, "Yeah, it's the yellow alright. The rest are okay. Is the perimeter line complete without yellow?"

The answer from the roof came back, "No, but I can splice it through."

"Okay then," said the man in charge. "Bypass yellow and we'll finish it, Thursday." Both workmen left the roof as we were being locked away in our cells. It was 5:00 pm.

+ + +

Our first night together, with three nights ahead of us, we discussed our legal problems and what chance Fritz might have of fleeing prison. Of course, I now knew that the remand alarm circuit, yellow, was disconnected until Thursday.

Fritz grew very excited when I told him of the security flaw, which in turn raised my hopes. I could not talk sensibly about court. My mind rejected it; instead, I kept circling the pro's and con's of escape. We mooted another plan.

While sitting on my bunk talking, Fritz had been idly scratching at the eastern wall near the locker, three besser-block courses up. To our surprise a large chunk of mortar came loose and fell in pieces to the floor. More out of curiosity than anything else, I picked up a piece to study… it was pumice stone, soap and bread!

We fingered out more, amazed, until one entire vertical course, 3-centimetres deep, was revealed to have been gouged out and cunningly re-packed with fake mortar to conceal the 'crime' of a hiding place.

Fritz and I had only envisaged the idea of exit via the barred window above the door, and then up through the yard's shroud of metal-mesh. But this audacious idea of penetrating a wall of stone was a punch in the brain, revealing a new vista of thought. A simply brilliant idea!

Remove a 20-centimetre by 40-centimetre besser block to expose the ex-chapel's west side—a 20-centimetre thick wall constructed of sandstone blocks—and, if penetrable, eventually gain access to the day-room which had a plaster ceiling easy to breach.

Then, up into the roof that we knew extended beyond the remand section to possible freedom. The day room's door was padlocked each night when the cells were sealed, and re-opened each morning when we were let out. The personal risks were high, but not unduly so if care and patience were exercised. It could be done.

Fritz carried, concealed in a flap of his cardboard box, a small stainless-steel knife that he removed to test the mortar. The blade scraped it away with reasonable ease while I stood lookout on the chair at the door, watching the brightly lit gate opposite for any sign of an approaching screw on patrol.

In less than an hour, Fritz had removed the top course of the forty-centimetre block, inwards to a depth of about three-centimetres. Then his progress was stopped. A persistent metallic sound kept coming from the groove. Fritz asked me to take a look.

A brick-tie was stopping the knife's entry. Disappointed, I slumped down, saying, "Unless those wires can be cut, you'll never get that block out of the wall."

Fritz persisted, scraping at the mortar. My confidence wasn't in it any longer, but I still kept lookout for him. Casually, I glanced out the window into the yard—a screw at the gate, coming in! The shock—it made me spring off the chair, a sprinter from his block.

The chair almost toppled, righting itself with a thump as I touched Fritz. Frantic, I rolled the small locker to him. My heart hammered, erratic, and my breath came in short gasps.

Fritz sprang up and grabbed his box, pretending to rummage for something. I sat quickly, nervously, on the toilet bowl with my back to the door, my neck muscles tense. A faint metal sound signalled that the spy hole had opened... then... an age later, a louder noise. He was testing the padlock on the day-room door.

Very cautiously, I stepped up onto the chair, my pulse slower and senses heightened now that action was required. Waiting is always the hardest. I watched him spy into the other cells, leave the yard and lock the gate.

Fritz resumed gnawing at the wall. Fifteen minutes later, the light went out; it was 10:00 pm. On the bottom bunk I lay, gazing at the vertical shadows cast by the bars, trying to listen only to the piped-in Country music on the gaol-radio—while being aurally seduced by the sedulous scraping, grating, rasping sound of Fritz with the knife... till finally faced with the naked truth; I wanted to escape too!

Rolling off the bed, I took the knife from Fritz to study his progress. Both vertical mortar courses had been scraped out entirely, so, while Fritz soaked his swollen hands in the sink, I attacked the underneath course of the besser brick. In the dark we worked, constantly eying the gateway in turn, planning how to go about getting what we needed, but lacked.

WHILE BE-ING AURAL-LY SEDUCED BY THE SEDULOUS SCRAPING, GRATING, RASPING SOUND OF FRITZ WITH THE KNIFE

The wires had to be cut and to sever them we had to have a saw of some kind. Therefore, a second knife was vital to notch teeth into the one we already had. It would need to come from the kitchen to avoid alerting the screws. If one went missing off a meal tray they would put on a tantrum until it was found. And because there was no real way to camouflage the gouged out courses, we were merely going to stuff bread in and trust it to Fate by standing the small locker in front of the problem and hope that the searching screws would be fooled by the obviousness of it.

+ + +

At 11:00 pm the radio went silent. Its cessation of covering sounds raised the risk of our endeavour ten-fold; but we laboured on. By now, having adapted mentally as well as physically to the situation, I felt reasonably relaxed, though ultra-alert. Three times that night, patrolling screws spied into our cell, but we persisted—with success—till dawn. And it was not until then that the detritus was carefully swept up and flushed down the toilet. I washed myself thoroughly and went to bed, exhausted, favouring bruised palms and cramped muscles. We lay there, incapable of speech and sleep, to eventually be roused at 6:30 am by the wake-up bell, cell-light and radio.

Fritz changed his knife's hiding place before let-out, from his box to the wall. That way, in case of the holes discovery (and search of our property) we could hotly deny knowledge of the damaged wall; we were clean. Additionally the few law books we had were stood on the locker's top, leaning against the wall to psychologically deter any randomised movement of the locker during the search to come. We knew that it only had to be moved a few centimetres and discovery would be inevitable! The door unlocked and the morning meal was given out. Our breakfast in the yard was uneventful and so was the period up to lunch—we slept through it in the warm sunshine.

+ + +

After lunch, we moved an old church pew from where it sat in the day room, voicing the excuse of poor light, to a place against the wall near our cell. Another step ahead: the bench would conceal any unintended damage done to the wall from the cell side. Shower time would be the litmus test; when they took us away and, in our absence, conducted the daily search. I thought I had accepted the dangers with equanimity but, when I heard the call to line up for showers, my jumping heart proved me false.

Gathering up my toiletries I stood first in line and Fritz waited at the rear. One was then in position to cause a diversion for the other if necessary. Also, if quick, the first into the shower would be back in the yard not long after the last had departed. This gambit we hoped, would hurry up the searchers.

Earlier in the day when the lunchtime meals were being distributed, I had created an opportunity to talk with the old lag who had brought us our meals each day, taking the chance of asking him to tape a knife in the groove of the evening meal's tray. Admittedly it was a big gamble to take, but so was the breach in the wall! The whole thing had gathered a momentum of its own. Besides, I learnt long ago that an essential ingredient for success—is audacity.

With my shower over, I rushed back to the yard and, as I went in, the bustled searchers filed out. I could see, while breathing out a long sigh of relief, that our cell had barely been touched. Towelling my hair and beard, I slowly relaxed while strolling up and down the yard waiting for the dinner tray, with the knife I hoped for, to arrive. The next hour crawled by.

✦ ✦ ✦

The meal's arrival caused me a pang of doubt—a young lout carried the tray, not the old crim. I visually counted off the knives… five only. Then I furtively fingered the groove. As I surmised: nothing!

With a screw listening nearby, I casually enquired,

"Where's the old guy today?"

And the reply, "He went sick to his slot and asked me to do it for him," only confirmed my suspicions.

Feigning disinterest, I stepped away from him to wait for the kitchen screw to hand out the meals and cutlery. We took our dinners and Fritz, being vegetarian, got his regular salad heaped up high with lettuce leaves. The tray, as usual, was sat on the step near the gate for the used utensils. That's when I would have palmed the knife.

Disappointed, I ate my stew sitting alone, wondering what the authorities would make of my knife request, presuming that the old lag had told them. They might move Fritz now, just when it seemed hopeful for us both. Unhappily, I watched Fritz nibble on his rabbit food and paw his plate, then go with it into our cell. When he returned a few minutes later chewing on a carrot, his plate empty, I quickly forgot it. Muster was called and, we were again secured for the night.

+ + +

As soon as the door slammed firmly shut, I began explaining how the knife deal had soured. Interrupting me and without further explanation, Fritz rolled the locker aside to expose the damaged wall. Reaching down, he came back up holding an old knife. "It was in my salad," he gleefully stated.

"That crafty old bastard!" I exclaimed. He had manipulated the lout into running the risk (unwittingly I'll bet!), alibiing himself from the knife in case of detection. And sending the knife through the salad warned Fritz of me wanting a weapon if my given reason was false. In complying, he had covered all the bases, yet kept 'crims faith' with me by the delivery! I now owed him a return favour. So go the rules of prison.

We were realistic enough to recognise that the aegis of luck could not be relied on and to agree that the hole had to be completed before Thursday. We had to gamble the-lot for the-lot, to have any chance. While Fritz watched the gate I sat on the bunk holding the knives, forcefully striking the blades together up and down their lengths till I was satisfied that both knives had been converted into primitive hacksaw blades. Sliding one under the pillow and gripping the other, I moved the locker to test the theory.

Fritz sprang off the chair as he hissed, "Two screws are coming in!" And shoved the locker to me.

Galvanised, I jumped—the clatter of keys rang clear as I thrust the knife, handle down, into the back of my briefs. Eyes searched and mind raced, needing something to copy the earlier sound of the knives. This was not a regular cell check with two of them at the gate! In despair, I wrenched a button from my shirt to strike the metal top of the locker as I pushed it to hide the hole, striking it to the musical beat on the radio. Fritz joined in by clapping.

Neither dared venture a look at the door. We were being observed. I could *feel* it. My pulse clamoured; anxiety played with my lungs. At long

SENDING THE KNIFE THROUGH THE SALAD WARNED FRITZ OF ME WANTING A WEAPON

last, the song ended. I stopped the infernal tapping to use the respite as an excuse to visit the toilet. Standing there with my penis dangling—hoping to embarrass—I glimpsed the Judas-hole slowly shut. Cautiously, on the chair I climbed to spy out the window.

Both screws were whispering, heads together, looking our way. I reached with my toes and flushed the toilet, miming for Fritz to make some noise. He commenced singing the German National Anthem! They shook their heads as they left, re-locking the gate. I jumped down and a nervous laugh released our pent up state. Our consensus was that a patrolling screw, or worse a prisoner, had reported the unusual sound of the knives.

We prepared ourselves mentally with a few well-chosen insults—and after a cold wash at the sink I again set myself to test the wire. A score of strokes and… it worked! Though the price was a harsh sound each time I stroked the blade. It set my nerves on edge. To be workable, it had to be faster and much quieter. There were eight wires to be cut: four on the top of the block and four on the bottom. If the wires were not severed before the radio went silent; it would be impossible to continue.

I quickly found that the spacing of the teeth on each blade was critical as they caused unnecessary noise and extra work; so by judiciously adding a few extra nicks to even out the teeth, I quietened down the sawing noise to teeth-gritting level. The speed of cutting also improved. The first wire—slightly thicker than a match—took me more than thirty minutes of experimenting to cut. The second wire took only half the time. We exchanged places.

That night we were spied on twice more before lights-out at 10:00pm. The visits were routine and not in response to our endeavour. In all, six wires were successfully severed before 11:00pm—with two still uncut.

Normally the radio switched off one hour after the lights went out; but for some reason unknown to us, the radio stayed on that night—until after midnight. If it had not, the plan would have foundered there. But now, with the additional hour of music to blanket our sawing, we were able to complete the removal of the besser-block before the new day began. That was the first rung up the ladder to freedom.

Lighting a match, expectant, I pushed the flame into the cavity. Revealed on the inside was exactly what we anticipated: the day room's wall, separated by a 10-centimetre gap. Tentative stabs with a knife at the sandstone wall confirmed that it was still a tenable plan. Pieces broke out, though not easily, proving that the stone was penetrable with the few tools in our possession. Time, and not material, was now the governing factor. Each large sandstone block we estimated to be 45-centimetres by 60-centimetres and at least 15-centimetres thick—impossible to remove the way we did the besser-block. The only feasible way for us to penetrate the wall in the time available was by drilling. But not with the knives: they were useless for the task. A core-drill was the only practical way for us to accomplish it and fortunately, the means of making such a tool stood close at hand.

The rear leg of the tubular steel chair twisted off easily, leaving a jagged edge at the broken end and a rubber grommet at the other. Cloth strips torn from a sheet were tightly bound over the end for grip. Putting the jagged end to the sandstone, I twisted it left and right in quick succession, pushing my weight into it. Only a minute of screwing it about and the drill had penetrated a centimetre into the stone! An excited nod to Fritz as a thrill of elation coursed about my body. We grinned foolishly at each other in the dimly lit cell.

We envisaged a rectangle of holes guided by the perimeter of the removed besser-block's cavity, with each hole to be bored outward at a 45 degree angle from the edge to ensure a conical tunnel for easier exit when completed. The drill was marked to indicate a depth of 15-centimetres to prevent any possibility of breaking out the other side; but if it did the pew was already in place to hide it.

The first hole took thirty minutes to drill. The next hole—3-centimetres higher up—took twenty minutes, and so did the third hole. I calculated... at least thirty holes could be bored in ten hours. To that add on fatigue, interruptions and different styles. Never the less, if Lady Luck kept on favouring us, it could be done by Thursday morn'!

We continued on, with me starting a fourth hole into the sandstone. Keys at the gate warned me even before Fritz did. The locker quickly concealed the hole before I slipped into the ready-made bed of the bottom bunk. Fritz stood at the toilet-bowl, head down, pretending to urinate. We had a routine now. In the time that it took a screw to peer in on us we were paragons of innocence. And though my pulse often quickened and I tasted bile a lot that night, there was never any real threat of discovery. Alternately, I stood vigil while Fritz worked on the wall and, so doing, I'd found where a narrow beam of light pierced the door above the small trap door built into it. A much better position to watch from— it's no fun standing on a three-legged chair half the night!

Each time the drill blunted, I'd shroud myself in blankets

to notch and tear the end with a knife, careful to minimise sound. Unfortunately the leg wore down faster than anticipated, making the work more difficult, so to maintain the gruelling pace we had set ourselves, I broke off the chairs remaining rear leg. Our hands were blistered, bruised and swollen but, when finally the cell was lit up with pre-dawn light, I counted twenty-four holes!

Into the cavity went the knives, and the brick was replaced. The chair legs were re-attached by inserting rolls of stiffened cardboard into the leg ends, and then into the stubs the legs were wrenched from. And woe-be-gone any screw so sloth-like as to sit on it during the next search! (Of course the report would assert that custodial acumen and diligence was what thwarted a brilliantly conceived escape attempt by two master criminals; where as in reality this miscast serious-comedy stumbled on, denied the benefit of a script.)

I washed up and no sooner had I fallen on to the bunk than the cell light glowed—indicating time to rise—accompanied by the raucous, but helpful, radio.

And another day of wits began.

✦ ✦ ✦

All that day, Tuesday, I sat beset with tension and experienced only brief, fitful naps—naps which left me more fatigued and irritable than if I had baby-sat six pre-schoolers for a week! And when the inevitable call for our showers came, Fritz and I waited at the gate, watching each other from opposite ends of the line, trying to appear nonchalant, not wanting to go out, but accepting that we had no choice if we were to maintain appearances.

With my shower over, I fretfully returned to the yard. The very first thing I saw on entering—sending a hot spasm of shock into my bowels—was the chair, one leg splayed out, standing there forlorn and askew in the centre of the cell! But when I entered to find the locker still standing sentinel in the aftermath of the search, my scrotal ache relented. Our incredible luck still held. If we'd been found out, by now I would have been under a hail of batons and abuse.

Straightening up the chair, I hung my wet towel over its back; then after folding our blankets, casually settled down in the yard to await Fritz. The next thing I recall is being shaken awake for the evening meal. I felt mentally numb and extremely tired; but the hour of deep sleep had left me calm and ready for the exertion of the night's work still to come.

+ + +

After the gate outside clanged shut and the rattle of keys had faded, I made my bed, not expecting to sleep in it, but soon to make it look like I was. A cell check by two screws had occurred every night between 11:00 pm and midnight (the change-over of shift) and there was no reason to suppose it would be any different this night. So we therefore intended to break through into

OUR INCREDIBLE LUCK STILL HELD. IF WE'D BEEN FOUND OUT, BY NOW I WOULD HAVE BEEN UNDER A HAIL OF BATONS AND ABUSE.

the day room after they had been and gone. But first, six more holes had to be drilled, plus the last few centimetres on each of the twenty-four holes, before their inspection. That allowed us six hours of toil to prepare everything and hopefully, to snatch some rest too. Any problems we encountered after breaching the day-room wall would have to be overcome as they presented themselves—or dismal failure.

It began.

Together we wrenched off the remaining two chair legs, and then Fritz set to drilling while I kept nit at the door. That first hole of the night was worked at without rest until it broke out on the other side, 18-centimetres in depth. Five more like that one, we calculated, plus twenty-four times 3-centimetre to ream out equalled 162-centimetres of sandstone to penetrate in less than six hours. Easy to do? A snack! Or so we thought.

The thirty holes were painfully completed before midnight. We slid the besser-block into its cavity, and then climbed tiredly into our bunks. All we waited for now was the bed check by the screws. Bone-weary, I lay there, sapped, devoid of lucid thought. And with each passing moment I grew more tired, trying desperately to stay awake. The need for healing sleep won: nirvana.

✚ ✚ ✚

The pain from my arm being twisted woke me. It was Fritz. The screws had been and gone, he said! I staggered to the sink. A short sleep, when emotionally and physically drained, is worse than no sleep at all. A zombian mentality, almost

impossible to shake, accompanied me to the wall. The sandstone had more holes in it than a piece of Swiss cheese; yet
still that stubborn substance refused to fracture! No wonder
it's such an outstanding building material. We had to drill out
more sandstone, levering and twisting in the holes with the
chair legs—till finally, *at last,* a tiny piece broke out. And that
was the beginning of the wall's demise.

More small fragments quickly broke loose into the cavity.
Then a large welcome chunk off the top row of holes broke
outwards, dropping loudly onto the wooden floor of the day
room. There was a hushed wait… but not for long! I thrilled
as I put my hand through and pushed the pew slightly away
from the wall. Rapidly now, the cavity widened as numerous
chunks fell away, feeding my urge to bolt so strongly that I
tried to squeeze out through it—and got stuck! The igno-
minious position sobered me. It took plenty of cold sweat
and skin before I was able to worm my head and shoulder,
back out. We laboured at widening it some more.

+ + +

Then Fritz tried it naked. He slid through quite easily, moving the pew out of the way for me to follow. But naked or
not, I could not slip through that hole. My chest was the
problem. If I could deflate it enough by exhaling and then
push myself into the opening—with Fritz on the other side
tugging my arms—I had a chance of getting through. Unfortunately, if I was wrong and I got stuck again, I would
very likely suffocate.

My confidence momentarily faltered, until I considered

the two alternatives: a long term of imprisonment if I stayed, or a chance of vindicating my assertion of innocence. Knowing that, I resolved to try it: to bust a rib in the attempt—or die.

Fritz wormed back into the cell and while he dummied-up his bunk, he listened as I described what I wanted him to do. Nit-keeping forgotten, we worked together to break away small protruding pieces of sandstone. Then he slid back into the day room.

I stripped off my clothes and lay a bed-sheet, folded in half lengthwise, through the bolthole. If I could force my arms and shoulders through, I could pull my chest free and naturally, the rest of my body would follow—I hoped.

Fritz readied himself. I lay on my back with my head and arms through the hole and took four deep breaths. With Fritz tightly gripping my wrists and his bum on the floor, his feet wide apart astride the hole, I gave the signal to begin. My trust in Fritz was well placed. Exhaling, I pushed HARD with both feet. He pulled and pulled my arms. Heart pounding, I almost made it with that first strenuous lunge. I exhaled more; my lungs burnt. A slight slip and I was almost birthed. I tried to say, "Pull harder," but all I wheezed out was a gasp. I couldn't breathe!

Fritz jerked my arms—to and fro—to no avail. In desperation, I wrenched my left wrist free of his limpet grip. He spun off balance, letting go my right. My elbows jammed against the wall, I tortuously pulled my chest free of the suffocating vice of stone. Deeply, I breathed in the cool night air, my rib-cage a ring of fire. I felt triumphant! Fritz whispered, "Are you able to get yourself out now?" His concerned look buoyed my spirit.

"Yes, Fritz," I whispered. "I'm alright now. But keep an eye on the gate," I cautioned him. "It must be after four."

Following that respite, I quickly worked the rest of my body out. There were a few aches and skin scrapes, but nothing to worry over. I changed places at the window with Fritz, to allow him to return to dummy-up my bunk and tidy the cell.

✝ ✝ ✝

Ten minutes of nervous waiting before he was back beside me with all my clothes and some incidentals of his in a bag (track-pants with the leg-ends tied off). The cell's locker again covered the gap. I cleared the stone bits away from the hole after dressing, and then pushed the pew against the wall to conceal our tunnel from spying eyes. Meanwhile, Fritz had been studying the high ceiling at the far end of the day room.

He stood a chair on the snooker table and climbed up to stab at the chalky plaster ceiling with a knife. A hole quickly developed, big enough to put his fingers in, to tear down a large pendulous strip. It made a crackling outcry that upset my composure; but it was necessary. Our time was rapidly running out. In only a few minutes (which of course seemed much longer) Fritz had opened the plaster wide enough to fit through. I watched him make two clumsy attempts to lift himself bodily into the ceiling. Before he could abort a third try, I dashed over and climbed on the chair under his dangling feet. He put them on my bent spine, pushed hard and disappeared into the roof.

While he worked above me to widen the rent, I re-turned the chair to the floor and hurriedly picked up all the big bits of fallen plaster; then clambered back onto the table with the bed-sheet from the hole. Fritz's hand reached down and I stretched up to take a firm grip. As he lifted me to the hole, I reached in with my free hand to grasp a roof-beam. With Fritz tugging, I easily entered the ceiling's musty maw. I felt elated and very, very much alive! Quickly, I lifted the hanging flap of plaster before tearing off a strip of bed-sheet, laying it under the flap to cover the breach and hold the plaster up.

At first it seemed pitch dark inside (and smelled of bird lime) but my eyes soon adjusted to the pinpoints of security-lighting entering in through tiny cracks and nail holes in the eaves. A crackling, brittle noise sounded from where Fritz crouched further along the ceiling. Stepping gingerly from beam to beam, I advanced to stand abut the eastern extrem-ity of the building. Peering down I saw through a hole Fritz was making, the prison's chapel lit by bright light from out-side the small chapel's large single window. I tied the sheet to a beam and, when the opening expanded enough, dropped its loose end into the room below. Feet first, Fritz squeezed through the plaster and slid down the sheet to a church pew. Handing down the bag, I followed him headfirst.

The chapel's floor measured 3-metre by 6-metre and the door, metal-clad and solid, was securely locked. A thick wire mesh on the outside protected the window. My joy faded. Out of one cell and straight into another! Outside the window a tennis court was visible, surrounded by the high-est walls I have ever had the dismay to greet. And perched in the far northeast corner of the court, a guard-tower watched with arc lights all round. I tasted the bitter bile of defeat.

Together we sat, disconsolate, both sadly agreeing that that was the end of it until… by staring through the lights of the hated tower we suddenly realised that it stood un-manned. Whether it was temporary or not, we had no way of knowing. But our hopes re-soared. Better to be caught in action, than kneeling on the executioner's-block waiting for the axe to chop.

Unlatching the window, I slid the glass panel up. Chill night-air entered the room. Fritz started sawing on a strand of wire near the top, while I sawed on the same strand at the bottom. The noise we made deafened my ears to all other sound; but time was running out and it was more important than caution. His wire broke first, followed by mine a moment later. The wire was springy and difficult to twist out; but when it did the rest concertinaed easily apart.

Without hesitation, Fritz squeezed through the slit clutching his bag. I adroitly followed to stand on the wet tennis-court drawing in air - air which now inexplicably smelt of freedom! The brightly illuminated yard, and the risk of danger, did not detract a whit from my pleasure of gazing up at the myriad of cloud-covered stars… thrilling to the soft, sensual touch of cold, misty rain on my flushed face! There is no doubt that deprivation definitely enhances one's appreciation!

I gazed about to locate Fritz, to share the moment. He was gone! I sprinted to the right without thought, away from the tower's menace, towards a high walled-in area with an open-gated passageway visible in its centre. I raced through expecting to find Fritz. With startling clarity I found myself in the sentenced-prisoner's section where a crim was being spied on by a peripatetic screw wrapped in a rain-cape and cap—only twenty metres away! Feeling trapped I stumbled back, out of sight, my heart pounding with fright. Bumping into someone behind me, I drove my elbow back, dropping down to sidekick and frightening Fritz (more than hurting him) with my reaction. He started to remonstrate—my adrenalin gushed—and desperately I hushed him and pantomimed the situation.

Accepting the risk, he entered the sports equipment enclosure; then came back out carrying a rolled-up tennis net and raced off towards the tower. I ran too, wondering how we were going to scale up to the tower without being sighted or caught. Or worse, shot by the patrolling turnkey somewhere behind us.

At the far end of the court, on the west side opposite the gun-tower, Fritz had disappeared from sight. A complete surprise… and a surge of new hope! I followed him through the wall, turned and pushed a steel gate closed behind me. Standing on wet grass looking about, my legs a-tremble in readiness, I faced a high east-west rectangular block of cells with their doors facing south: a modern section compared to the rest of the prison. Cautiously I peered through the second cell's peephole. It took me a minute to realise that what I saw was a sleeping woman! We were in the female section. I hurried to Fritz and warned him to be ultra-quiet.

He had dropped the tennis-net on the grass with his bag and was forcing open the last door, next to the narrow yard's west wall. It was a laundry and its wooden door posed no problem. He clambered up onto the door while I held it steady. But the roof's eave was beyond reach. I had to get up there too, which I quickly did. Fritz climbed up awkwardly onto my bent back and then, with me leaning against the wall, carefully stood on my shoulders. When his weight eased off my straining body, I breathed a sigh of relief before looking above. He hung precariously by his forearms. I dropped to the ground and closed the door in case he fell.

With great risk and effort he slowly worked his chest over the ledge. After that, he was safe. It took only a few tries before he struggled onto the roof and vanished from sight. I stepped back to the gate and stealthily eased it open. Crouched down, with my head near the sweet smelling grass, I peered out. The rain had stopped, making the arc lights seem extra bright. No screw was in sight and, as I re-closed the gate, some of the tension drained away. I returned to the bag and net to watch for Fritz to re-appear.

Crouched in silhouette, he appeared on the roof's edge and pointed at the net. I threw it up to him and he caught it on the second toss. One end he tied around his waist, sitting near the gutter's edge, then let the rest unroll to me. I attached Fritz's bag to the net and waited, anxious.

Responding to a whispered, "Climb up" from Fritz; I gripped the net. There were a few toe-slips on the wet wall, but nothing to faze or slow my determined ascent. Squatting on the roof, I peered through the prison lights at the distant houses and water-glistening roads, exultant in our success—so far. We both knew, lying there in silence, that it was not yet time to congratulate each other. Six metres of lethal fall still had to be safely negotiated to attain the outside wall: plus two alarm barriers. But another rung of our ladder to freedom had been scaled.

I spent myself mentally while Fritz removed his bag and secured the net to a small chimney on top of the laundry;

then he came back unrolling the net, to stand next to me on the west side of the roof in the northern corner. I knelt where the internal wall joined the outside wall, just four metres away. Both walls were the same height, and each one was topped with what looked like a small fence. They were, in fact, alarm sensors. Because it came from the men's section, we believed that the nearer one was remand-yellow and therefore dead; but if we were mistaken and it 'went off' on contact, we were prepared to scramble along the top of the north/south wall with the net and descend the outer wall with all haste. But if it remained silent, I was to crawl out alone to choose the best place to cross the live alarm.

I gathered up the net. Fritz again checked its anchor-end and slung his bag around his neck, ready. Except for the net, I stood unencumbered. With a nod from Fritz, I (more taut than a bow-string) took the first step onto the wall. Quickly straddling the wires, I waddled the few metres—with lawn below me on both sides of the narrow chasm—to halt just short of the lurking perimeter alarm. No siren had cried out. I sucked in a few deep breaths to relax my nervousness while Fritz stoically watched the gate as agreed. I felt a cockiness now, mentally alert and physically ready for any feat. I gazed down into a walled-in back yard of a house, connected to the prison via a sturdy narrow gate: the Superintendent's house for sure. Not a good place to drop into! I signalled Fritz to come out to me.

He saw the risk, as I did, of going over where we stood and the need to descend further along, beyond where the lower wall outside met the prison wall. When the alarm was to sound—and we KNEW it would—any additional barrier to overcome could be fatal. Taking the end of the net from me, Fritz held my belt while I gingerly reached over with my right hand to take a firm hold on the nearest alarm bracket affixed to the top of the penultimate rung on our ladder to freedom. Again... no alarm sounded. But this one I knew to be dormant and not dead like the one we still straddled. Resolute, I rolled off to hang two-fisted from the bracket on top of the six-metre high wall stretching eastward to the Janusian guard tower: my life in the balance. I reached to the next alarm bracket, and the next, and in that way I progressed about ten painstaking metres. Spiders had multiplied in my bowels. I looked to Fritz (my hands pained) but he waved me on further until, two metres along, he signalled me to stop. I released my left hand and stuck it out at a right angle. I hung precariously by my straining right hand, trying not to think of the drop beneath me.

Taking careful aim, Fritz threw the net and as it un-ravelled in the air, it fell neatly over the crook of my elbow. Metre by anxious metre, I pushed the net under the alarm wires... and soon the green mesh was stretched out behind me across the gap, from the wall to the laundry's little chimney. I waved to Fritz to come on out.

He gripped the first bracket as I had, swung out and hung there. He then did the same with the second. Grabbing for the third bracket in line, his hand reached too high. The bottom wire was touched, earthing the circuit, and the alarm clamorously SOUNDED!

Electrified, and without any conscious thought or ef-fort, I pulled up and rolled through the wires, to spin over and grip the net. The wall was rough. I went down it like an Olympic Gold finalist! My knuckles were skinned. I felt no pain. Every thing around me slowed down, except my heart—it raced!

Touching the soil at speed, I let go of the net and stumbled back a pace, only to somersault another metre down into rotting vegetable matter. Fritz loomed into view above. I floundered out of the heap as Fritz slid down the net. I loudly cautioned, "Be careful! There's rubbish beneath you," then ran towards a patch of bushes in shadow to the east of me, only a few paces away, to stare back and watch Fritz tumble the same as I did. Rolling over, he stood up and stumbled northwards.

I ran from the concealing shadows and headed east under the gun-tower, calling to Fritz over the wailing sound of the alarm, "Over here, Fritz! Follow me!" I loped over the grass, my heart pounding pain and my mouth bone dry. The hounding cadence of the prison alarm wailing behind me. I slowed my pace as I reached the prison's perimetre two-metre high cyclone-wire fence.

Over the fence I scrambled, running past school buildings to reach a poorly lit residential street. I halted to catch my breath and look back. Fritz was racing towards me across the schoolyard. The prison alarm could no longer be heard, and belied what must have been happening back there. I sped off again, down the shadow-side of a side street, travelling southwards to freedom. As I ran, my thumping heart slowed its frantic beat. A plumbeous weight took wing and a thrill of lightness filled me—a mercurial moment—actually giving vent to a shout of delighted joy!

Fritz escaped to regain his liberty; I escaped to prove my innocence. But at that moment—that moment of exuberant running—all I experienced was the sensual delight of being free. Free! Out FREE!

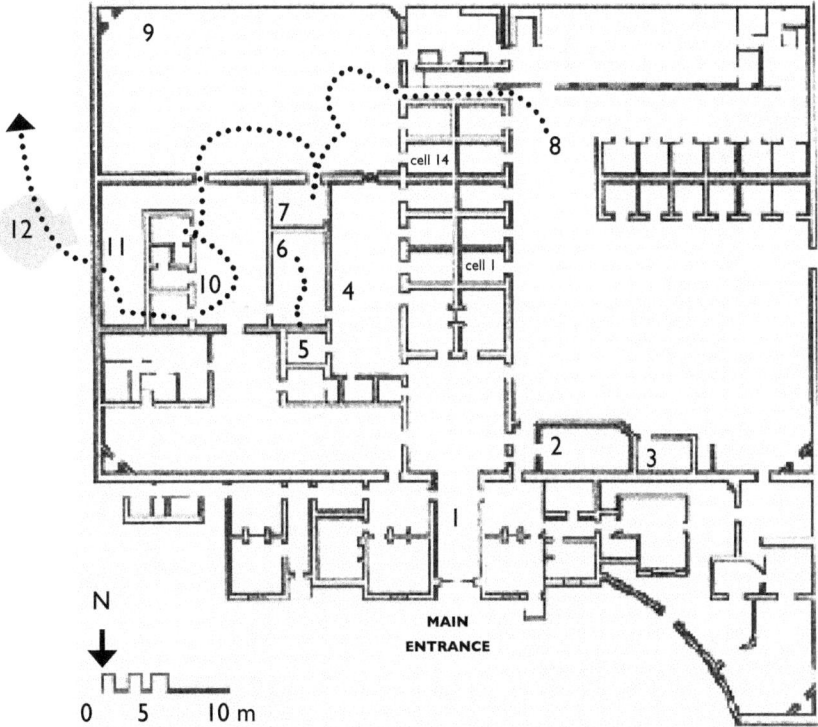

▼ Escape route from Mt Gambier gaol

1. Vehicle entrance
2. Superintendant's office
3. Shower
4. Remand yard
5. CELL
6. Hole in ceiling
7. Chapel
8. Screw on patrol
9. Tower
10. Climb to the roof
11. Alarm sounded
12. Pile of rubbish

CHASE

THE GREATEST PROVIDER OF ALL...

IS HOPE

THURSDAY 30TH NOVEMBER 1978
MOUNT GAMBIER, S.A

I sped down dark and wet streets. My pumping legs made me feel as if I could run forever! The feeling though, was soon marred.

"Joe!" Came Fritz's strident voice behind me. "Stop running, Joe."

Slowing to a brisk walk, I continued on. The air was cold and smelt clean.

"Wait!" Came another loud demand. "I must talk to you, now!"

"You can do that while we walk," I called back. "What do you want anyway?"

"We must steal a car," he urged. "Soon it will be morning

and we are not far enough." He touched my arm in an attempt to stop me.

"Don't you ever think!" I angrily snapped, shrugging his hand off. His carping had spoilt my thrill of fleeing the prison. I resumed running. It was imperative that we gain kilometres to outdistance a cordon.

I heard the plod of feet behind me so Fritz still adhered to my plan of putting the township between us and them—our inevitable pursuers—before sunrise. Without a stolen car report they MIGHT presume that a prearranged vehicle had picked us up and not bring in tracker-dogs. They were our main worry: we had no pepper, perfume, nor aniseed to break our scent.

Before escaping, I had carefully explained it all to him: how a hunted person was soon ruled by induction (rather than deduction) if fear and physical need were allowed to dominate the mind. While we ran, keeping to the shadows in each street, I searched the sky for the Southern Cross. It was crucial that we travel southwards through the city. The coast waited less than 30-kilometre south—a region planted with pine trees ranging the coastline for 50-kilometre or more—a most unlikely place for two city-reared prison escapees to head for, or so I reasoned.

Glimpsing the occasional glow of car lights in hills to the southwest, I followed the next few streets headed in their direction. I sustained the same steady jogging pace until the last street on the outskirts of the city was reached. Exhausted, we gratefully rested, while surveying the somnolent paddocks in the pre-dawn light, seeking a tree line to follow. Eventually we agreed on an old macadam road wandering through farmland; we would follow it till a suitable place was found to lie-up for the day and sit out the mongering bullshit always broadcast to agitate the locals.

Refocussed, we drank our fill again from a garden hose before continuing on. The damp grass quickly soaked our footwear as we loped silently over the thickly carpeted paddocks in Indian file, always keeping clear of any cattle and avoiding the few sentinel farmhouses with kitchen lights aglow. The morning breeze evaporated the perspiration on my face and body. I enjoyed the chill and our laboured breathing in no way indicated lack of fitness, simply an indication of the many twisting kilometres—and many days of unrelenting tension—put behind us that morning. Sun-up was less than one hour away.

✚ ✚ ✚

The post-dawn rays of light cast shadows to the right of us as we travelled. Occasionally farmers could be seen gathering in cows for their morning milking. We dared not risk a solitary sighting. Plodding along now, our ability to run gone, I missed the obvious. Pedantic Fritz brought it to my attention. "That place has many buildings, Joe. The broken one looks good to me." He asked, "What do you think?"

I thought it looked ideal, and said so. What I had mistaken for a coppice was actually the windbreak for a small group of buildings. A modern house stood abut to the road we were shadowing and at its rear were three large sheds. Off to the side, with its roof partly collapsed and overgrown with wild plant growth, stood the original farmhouse. If no dog barked, it would be ideal to hide in for the day.

From the rear we approached and cautiously entered by what was once the laundry. Two lights in the occupied house were visible from where we stood, and kitchen sounds came out to greet us. Provided we kept quiet and well hidden, there seemed to be no cause for concern; the place had a comfortable vibe about it. A filthy tap produced red rust, but within minutes we were able to quench our thirsts with long draughts of clear water. Then we re-arranged a small junk-filled room, with a half collapsed roof and no door, to provide us a cleared space to lie down, and material to block the doorway.

Prior to escaping, Fritz had been very enterprising. He produced from his bag a variety of things squirreled away: a pair of socks, a comb, soap and a face cloth. Returning from the tap, refreshed and dry-footed, I was surprised to find a small feast laid out to eat: sultanas, carrots, fruit, and chocolate no less! Fritz even had a transistor plugged into his ear. We ate, and after listening to the 6:30 am news (which made no mention of our escape) I plummeted into deep sleep—my very last thought being that the next bulletin would report our breakout. Shoot on sight! An escapee has no rights.

THE NEXT BULLETIN WOULD REPORT OUR BREAKOUT. SHOOT ON SIGHT! AN ESCAPEE HAS NO RIGHTS.

✛ ✛ ✛

I awakened... groggy and disorientated... to

voices shouting and the sounds of kids at play. The roof-beams above framed scudding clouds... and then I remembered! I sprang up to investigate. I quickly awoke Fritz and together we studied the barricaded doorway with the apprehension of exploring children in mind. A few gaps were filled in and we changed position for better concealment. With the earplug in his ear, Fritz tuned in the transistor. I relaxed, visualising

▲ Joe, Adelaide, 1987

ahead - but not too far. One step at a time with a defined objective. Plan too far and we risked failure. I had a peaceful ten minutes of lying there, gazing up at the sky, until Fritz touched my arm. He whispered, "In one minute, Joe, it will be four o'clock. And then the news." So that explained the kids: school's out for the day. I sat up to listen.

Fritz unplugged the earpiece to allow us to hear the broadcast together. "It has been confirmed that two dangerous prisoners escaped from the Mount Gambier Prison in the early hours of this morning. Prison authorities have not yet released their names, though it is known that the two men were on remand for safe-breaking offences. Police advise that they must not be approached. A car with Victorian licence plates was sighted near the prison and prison sources state the two could not have done it without outside assistance." What rubbish! I moved to the broken window. Misinformation like that only confused me; but the urge to listen was strong. Our escape was the culmination of luck, their laxity and our intestinal fortitude. To suggest other than that would be a lie.

Fritz intruded into my thoughts. "I have fruit, Joe. Would you like one?" He offered me a small orange.

While eating, we quietly laid plans for the advancing night. Relying on the lack of fact in the newscasts, we were reasonably safe in the area unless sighted, so our original plan remained unchanged: to reach Adelaide by way of a coastal route. And I promised Fritz a loan of half the money I had hidden to get him home to Sydney; but only if he abided by my travel condition—no major crimes were to be committed. Fritz agreed to that in principal. The money (a total of $2000) was in a jar hidden under the stove of a farmhouse I used to rent just prior to my arrest and frame-up.

+ + +

After a few more news updates the sun had set and the family next door settled in to their dinner, Fritz and I left as stealthily as we'd arrived, still heading south. The night air soon turned cold. Very cold. And when we halted for even a minute's rest, a clammy body-chill quickly set in. Moonlight kept the murky night away while we hiked along forgotten tracks through a forest of endless pine trees.

The temperature grew progressively colder as we trudged the rolling hills, until the bitter cold air forced us to halt at a derelict logging-cum-quarry railway siding. But as we were settling in to stay, a dog voiced it's warning; someone must have lived there, a woodcutter or a watchman perhaps. We quickly scrounged around and found four plastic bottles that we filled with rainwater from a tank; then moved on.

✚ ✚ ✚

An hour of more weary travel—and our limbs were again painfully frozen. At the next quarried cutting, we dropped down into a moonlit hollow and built two delightfully warm fires to stand between. Fritz materialised articles that were invaluable to us: a prison's steel water jug packed with instant coffee and Nestle milk. Even a spoon to measure it with! We quickly boiled water and made some strong, sweet, rejuvenating coffee. Our bodies rapidly thawed. Within an hour we were ready to go.

Before setting out, we each filled a bottle with hot black coffee to clasp to our bodies for warmth. Accompanied by Fritz and his blaring transistor, with Crux in the heavens to guide us, I set out again with renewed vigour and hope. We eventually reached a highway and followed it westward. Every approaching headlight we avoided like the plague, hiding from sight until it was safe to trudge on, and enduring the fatigue till finally we entered a small sleepy town.

Unfortunately my intention to pass through it, unseen and unheard, was thwarted by Fritz wanting to steal a car. The boots he wore had seriously chafed his feet. We had tramped over fifty blistering kilometres (pun intended) in two swift nights. Our differing priorities caused us to part

there. I took a bottle and topped it up with tap water, put a handful of raisins in my pocket and set out alone, walking along a train-track that skirted the town, headed west. I felt disloyal to Fritz, and unhappy over the abrupt parting but, resolute, I had set my mind not to aggravate my cause, no matter the cost.

To walk a train-line for any great distance is physically demanding. And stepping from sleeper to sleeper—an unnatural shortened step—numbs the mind and methodically slaughters the feet; but I willed myself to persevere. Walking a train-track is more direct and safer than a road any day! Disjointed imagery ricocheted inside my brain-cells, becoming more jumbled with each hobbled step along that skull-jarring track. The hours jostled by until finally, surcease came when the rising sun sent its warming rays over the frigid land. At last I could rest.

A rocky railway cutting revealed a narrow cleft overgrown by a leafy bush and after crawling in, I built a nest in which to snooze the day away. Yet as I lay there numbed by fatigue, desperately seeking sleep, my jangled mind still tramped that train-track! I wet my shirt-tail and washed myself all over. I then lay comfortable in the warm sun that filtered through the canopy of green leaves and slowly masturbated. Puerile or not, it swept me off to the land of Nod: into a dreamless, recuperative sleep.

+ + +

Later... the sun well past its zenith... I awoke to the harsh beat of a small aeroplane buzzing the cutting, very low overhead. But shrugging it off, I calmly drifted back to sleep. The day was almost gone when next I awoke. However, it was to throbbing feet and an aching back. My mind was crystal clear. Eating the remainder of the raisins and finishing off the water, I massaged my sore feet till the sun set when I again set out, tramping the tracks westward. Each step sent messengers of pain.

I WOULD TRAVEL WEST BY THE FASTEST MEANS AVAILABLE TO ME TO ELUDE THE LOCAL MANHUNT

+ + +

Hours later, tired and freezing cold, the glittering lights of a large township could be seen beckoning ahead. I followed the first paved roadway the tracks crossed, which led me into the outskirts of the city, to stealthily seek out what I sought: a lock-up garage with a car in it. I soon located one.

Slipping a strip of plastic torn from my water bottle into the jamb of the garage's side door, I wriggled the lock's tongue back, springing it open. I closed the door securely behind me and inspected the car. All the doors were locked, but that was no worry. A cursory search of the garage got me a coat hanger that I straightened out, leaving the hook to push down between the glass and rubber of the driver's door, to engage the bar and lift the button. Inside, I turned down the radio's volume control before switching it on to tune in the local radio station. All I wanted was the latest news.

Soft music gradually relaxed me. While waiting, I checked out the vehicle and, except for a packet of chewing gum and a blanket to wrap round myself, I left all else alone. Then the 3:00 am bulletin voiced forth and the part that reversed all my good intention, was the following: "It has been officially confirmed that the Mount Gambier Prison escapees were in fact hiding in the region until yesterday. Police report they are armed with a rifle and travelling in a cream station wagon, registration . . " I tuned my thoughts out, fuming! Fritz must have unwittingly stolen a car with a rifle in it. The hunt would now be stepped up. The best course for me, I theorised, was to make the most of Fritz's mistake.

I was irresolute at first: then I made the decision. I would travel west by the fastest means available to me to elude the local manhunt—by the very car in which I sat. I recalled seeing keys in the bottom of the glove box, so got them out to use as a fake set. And surprisingly, they were the car's spare keys! The petrol gauge registered half a tank.

I raised the tilt-up door and slowly pushed the heavy car out (a ten minute effort in itself) rolling it down the driveway to the street before starting up. At the townships centre, road signs pointed to three possible destinations: Kingston, Penola, and Mount Gambier. Along the Kingston road, I travelled west. The township dwindling behind me was Millicent: a tiny distance from Mount Gambier on any road map. But for me it had been a harrowing, worrisome journey!

+ + +

As each kilometre fled behind me in that comfortably heated car, buoyancy grew within, lifting my waning spirit; the radio's jaunty music lessened my feeling of loneliness. At last, I felt that I was going to make it. Two small towns quickly passed me by... though soon the petrol gauge forced me to make another decision. Without money and still in prison-garb, my choices were limited: did I exchange the car for one with a full tank; steal petrol; or continue driving till the petrol ran out and then resume walking? A broad semi-desert region—the Coorong's—still waited for me and had to be traversed to reach Adelaide. A road-sign appearing in my headlights decided for me. It said, Robe.

I took the turn-off and followed it to the outskirts of a fishing town where, on a vacant hectare, I concealed the car behind thick scrub. I skulked about in nearby house-yards until I found a large petrol drum and a length of garden hose to siphon with. I stole fuel out of a truck's tank then found another drum to fill. It drizzled cold rain but my nerves and activity kept me warm. A few hurrying cars passed by and an alert dog barked at me, but my determination saw me safely back to the car with the petrol intact.

Before departing, I returned the hose and drums to leave as little evidence of the 'crime' as possible. Only an hour or so of darkness was left. I drove rapidly back to the Princess Highway via Kingston, to begin the 100 kilometre risk-fraught passage through the Coorong's. The further I drove the more tense I became, with Spinifex and Saltbush on one side of the highway and unrelenting ocean on the other. Five cars caught me up, and passed; then the sun rose quickly in the sky. I didn't like the dawning.

Worried now, I watched for a place, any place, to conceal the car and sleep the sun away. And then I saw in the rear-view mirror a rapidly approaching vehicle, which stole my breath away. The first sighting of a police-van set my heart thumping and my stomach wrenched. A feeling of dread, steeped in failure, washed over me. There was nothing I could do on that dismal stretch of coastal highway. Except do nothing!

The patrol wagon sat behind, pacing me; then pulled out to draw alongside. The driver stared at me (an hour in subjective time) and I gave a rictus smile back. He studied 'my' car… then roared his vehicle ahead. Not until he disappeared around a bend ahead did my aching groin untwist. I swung onto the very next track inland and raced the car along it into a low spot. Hastily, I gathered a blanket, water and other items together; then hiked a few quick kilometres inland to get as far from the car in case of a search. The copper might later match my description, or licence-plate number, and get a search-plane up.

In the gnarled roots of an old gum tree, I curled up, and fell instantly to sleep.

+ + +

The screech of a hawk woke me. It was almost dusk. I sat there in the shade of the tree that had protected me all day, watching the sun sink, though I wasn't prepared for the charcoal night that suddenly blanketed me. Stumbling about confused in the dark, I head-

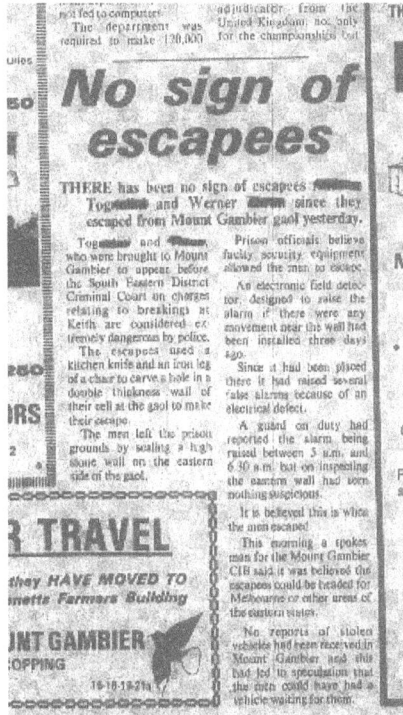

No sign of escapees

THERE has been no sign of escapees Tog----- and Werner ----- since they escaped from Mount Gambier gaol yesterday.

Tog----- and -----, who were brought to Mount Gambier to appear before the South Eastern District Criminal Court on charges relating to breaking at Keith are considered extremely dangerous by police.

The escapees used a kitchen knife and an iron leg of a chair to carve a hole in a double thickness wall of their cell at the gaol to make their escape.

The men left the prison grounds by scaling a high stone wall on the eastern side of the gaol.

Prison officials believe faulty security equipment allowed the men to escape.

An electronic field detector, designed to raise the alarm if there were any movement near the wall had been installed three days ago.

Since it had been placed there it had raised several false alarms because of an electrical defect.

A guard on duty had reported the alarm being raised between 5 a.m. and 6.30 a.m. but on inspecting the eastern wall had seen nothing suspicious.

It is believed this is when the men escaped.

This morning a spokesman for the Mount Gambier CIB said it was believed the escapees could be headed for Melbourne or other areas of the eastern states.

No reports of stolen vehicles had been received in Mount Gambier and this had led to speculation that the men could have had a vehicle waiting for them.

▲ Newspaper clipping about the escapees from 30 November 1978

ed for the dim glow of occasional car-lights on the horizon.

The moon eventually rose to cast its light over everything, enabling me to locate the car. It sat in shadow and the sky was overcast, so I approached it with caution in case of a stakeout, using scrub and shadow to advantage. There was an animal's scurrying sound near the car when I opened the door—I missed a heartbeat, or four—but soon I was back on the coast highway, again speeding west in style. The farmhouse where my hoarded savings were secreted was 30 kilometre south of Adelaide in rolling hills near Willunga and, to get there, I had opted to cross the Murray river at Wellington where a ferry service operated: a district I knew reasonably well.

+ + +

Hours later, with mixed feelings of relief and new worries, I drove on to the ferry and crossed over without a problem; I even talked with the ferry-man about local weather and the time: 10:30 pm and cold.

The drive from the ferry to Meadows was long and tiring. I had switched off the heater and wound down the window to keep me awake, and by about midnight, I turned at last into tree-lined Myponga road, with only the last few minutes of three gruelling days to go to retrieve my money. A frisson, like coming home, lifted me emotionally.

The turn-off for the farmhouse waited a few curves ahead on the hilly road. I slowed the car to prepare for it. But as I took the last bend, a hot flush of fear banished all feelings of homecoming from my heart. A station wagon pointed across the roadway into my lane with its passenger door agape; the interior light haloed a uniformed copper behind the wheel staring out through the open door. And starkly lit, in the centre of my headlights, was a second uniform holding his left hand up high in a halt sign! Clutched in his right fist was a large revolver, partly obscured by his thigh.

My mind raced into the red! Automatically, I dipped the lights and slowed the car. My heart-valves fluttered. Engaging first gear, I actually drew past him before stopping. My knees shook. It had all happened so quickly, yet my thoughts were still functioning in the clear.

The gun didn't bother me unduly—but the block-car did. If its motor was running (and I presumed it to be) the driver had only to jump it forwards a metre to cut me off. A steep embankment on my right and a sloping drop to my left destroyed all thought of evasive driving. To stand any chance of racing by, I had to edge closer.

My car crept forward. To allay the suspicions of the passed uniform, I offered, "Can I help you, Constable?" Trying my earnest best to project concern. "Has there been an accident?"

The Constable spoke loudly, very civil. "Please turn off the motor, sir. I wish to speak with you." He stepped towards me.

"Is something wrong, Officer?" Lifting the clutch slightly, my foot twitched with barely controlled nerves as the car inched forward. "Can I be of help?" I smiled a poor copy of confidence.

He lunged and grabbed the door, demanding, "Stop this vehicle, now!" All civility gone from his voice. "And turn the motor off!"

Feigning fright, I cried, "Alright, Constable! Take it easy!" I reached for the keys, blank-minded. I had no intention of turning off the ignition, but I clutched at any straw like a drowning man, to delay the inevitable. The police car still sat too far away for me to zoom past.

Then without premeditation, intuitively, I called out distinctly to the cop in the car who had watched my every move: "A policeman has been hurt!" I pointed back the way I had come. "I think he's been shot!"

My shouted non-sense worked. As the driver slid across to the passenger-side of the seat (per-

THE CAR CATAPULTED AWAY, ENGINE SCREAMING. AND IF A SHOT WAS FIRED, I CERTAINLY NEVER HEARD IT.

haps to hear better from the open door) I lifted the clutch and tramped the accelerator!

"It's him!" Shouted the constable holding my door. "It's him!" As I jerked him off his feet. The car catapulted away, engine screaming. I rode the clutch mercilessly. And if a shot was fired, I certainly never heard it.

I careered around the next curve before their car moved. It wasn't my intention to try and out-race them, knowing the area enough to know that a car chase was suicide—I had a better chance on foot. I glimpsed their lights fishtail behind me.

At the next dip in the roadway I slammed the car to a halt and jumped out—to scramble up the embankment away from the open paddocks on the opposite side. A many-strand wire fence halted me. Scaling it, I detected a rubber hose fitted along the top strand: a stud farm! I now knew where I was.

Over flat land I sprinted northwest, away from the car behind me. To my right reared a hill and to my left was soot black. A yelping, barking sound chilled me. I faltered. They had a dog with them to sool on me!

Fright spurred me on, only to sprawl face first in a stinking mud creek. I heard the dog getting closer, barking excitedly, and homing in on my floundering exit from the muck. After climbing out I encountered a second fence, painful and unexpected. I sprang up and over it, to receive a mild shock of electricity as I landed on the other side. I yelled out in fright. And bolted.

A trickle of moonlight chased away the stygian night. I was running between two hills, the left one precipitously steep. Turning to it, I started to climb. The dog barked madly, thwarted by the second fence on the creek, while the police called to each other. Torches flashed. I climbed till, exhausted, I stumbled and continued to climb more. My lungs were on fire and my heart demanded rest.

When the moon came out of the clouds in its full glory—the scene unfolding below me less than 100 metres away—I rolled onto my back, virtually standing upright, to do some yoga discipline, easing my aching heart and twitching leg muscles, beseeching the moon to hide again.

A cry of pain and fright flew up from below, with the anxious words from further back, "Hold him, Tom. Hold him! I'm nearly there." The electric fence had obviously shocked one of them too!

I lobbed an egg-sized rock down the gully, away from where I hugged the hillside. There was an eternity of tension in fear of them looking up... and then the soft thud of the rock's arrival far away. The dog barked—and dashed for the stone with the other two tailing! I finished the killing climb to arrive at a point overlooking the search area of which I was the hunted quarry.

✚ ✚ ✚

Cars were converging on the creek from three points. To me, that meant that the farm's patch had been staked out. I ran towards big power pylons to the north-west of me barely visible on the skyline. I bound down the long sloping hill and then up the other side through a field studded with hay bales. Distance was the governing factor now. If I failed, I'd be encircled—and flushed out later. I forced myself to run.

A set of lights on Myponga road seemed to pace me. And when they turned in to illuminate the hill-slopes ahead, I feared my run had been to no avail. That car, with another behind it, was entering the access track to the power-lines for which I strove. Unless I crossed that track first, I would be encircled. Frantic, I tried harder. If I failed to reach it, it was over for me. The pounding pace sapped my distressed body of energy; the steep slope angled me down, inexorably, towards Myponga road. Both police cars, our paths converging, clawed and jerked their way up the steep grade. My heart about to burst, I plunged on.

They beat me! The first car advanced past, straining on up the broken track towards the crest. The second car stopped below me, its lights ablaze. I collapsed prostrate, trembling from exertion, almost sick, and awash in sweat. The lower car started to move again—I perked up, alert to any chance offered, and crawled in nearer to the track. The headlights of the labouring vehicle momentarily pointed skywards as it spat gravel and edged up onto a rocky outcrop. A patch of deep shadow concealed the track near me. I sprinted across, expecting to hear a shot (or at least a shout) but nothing came. I tripped and sprawled flat.

The headlights settled back on the dirt and the car's straining engine died. Partly concealed, I lay in a pile of leafy debris, lit by the edge of the left headlight beam. I could hear the staccato sounds of the police radio, then a few of their comments:

"Do you think he's armed?"

"Nah. They caught the Kraut with the rifle."

"It might not be him then, eh?"

"Who else could it be."

"Are you gunna waste him if he comes this way?"

"I've never shot anyone. The star force'll get him; that's their job."

The police radio interrupted them with a brief traffic of words. Then the car clawed another fifty metres up the hill. A third car turned onto the track and climbed a hundred metres to stop, picketing the area with the other two further up. A classic type of encirclement—except that I wasn't in it!

Carefully now, I picked my way down the thinly wooded slope to where the land levelled out near Myponga road. Nestled there out of sight, I discovered a dam where I submerged my head and arms in the frigid water, sucking in small gulps to assuage my hot thirst.

Laying back to rest, I spewed it all back up, my stomach cramped in pain. I thought about Fritz and the significance of what I had overheard. He must have been caught in a trap set for me at the farmhouse. We really are creatures of habit, especially under stress.

I climbed the hill to reconnoitre. A horde of lights was gathering in the area around and to the north of 'my' car. Special Tactical Armed Response (STAR) was involved; dogs, guns, and a score of police were already there. What next and why!? Was all of this normal procedure to hunt for an unconvicted escapee charged with stealing? Not murder! Not rape. Not even armed robbery! Or was it fear of exposure now that I had my freedom to talk to the press!

+ + +

The farmhouse was south of Myponga road. I had to get to it. Denied money, I would be at the mercy of my needs; so I had to cross over and try for my $2000, but it wouldn't be easy. Two divisional vans were patrolling the roadway a kilometre or so back and forth, flashing their spotlights everywhere. Psychology intended to deter any attempt by me to cross over—which decided me to try!

Sneaking over to the barbed-wire fence skirting the road, I eased out through it, to very carefully peer down a two-metre drop to glistening black bitumen below. The southern side revealed flat dairy-farm paddocks, gradually rising to an uncleared section in the distance. The wire fence opposite bristled with rampant blackberry bushes. I crawled along the embankment seeking a gap in the berry growth and, when I spotted one, sat myself down to wait. The patrolling cars cruised by a few more times, and soon I had the pattern. I set my mind to act on it.

The first car cruised by... then the second car passed. I dropped down and bounded across the road. Heart pounding, I dove into the gap and over the fence to drop painfully behind the blackberries, my hands torn and bleeding. The picket cars returned, their spotlights searching.

After they passed by, my heart rate slowed a bit. I now had the problem of the open field to cross. By uprooting a small leafy bush to suit the need, I began to retreat from the net, holding it to obscure my shape whenever the moon broke through or a spotlight cast about. The wet grass chilled me to the bone.

At the trees, I made a running beeline for the farm: a house with a few dilapidated sheds surrounded by gnarled pine trees, waiting less than a kilometre away. Unpursued, my step felt lively and the exercise warmed me. Near the un-lit house, I cautiously crept in close and listened—the 'filth' could be lurking inside. I allowed an hour to elapse before I was satisfied that its ambience felt right. Then I moved in.

Like a cat burglar, I raised the kitchen window, centime-tre by slow centimetre, till it was open enough for me to slip undetected into the house. The kitchen was ink black. I knelt on the lino-floor and crawled stealthily over to the stove. At its base, I silently removed a house-brick and ferreted out my cash; I then carefully replaced the brick.

Outside again, I quietly closed the window before leav-ing, headed south away from the police cordon to the north, carrying one hundred twenty-dollar notes in my pocket. I was famished, and not a pie-cart in sight!

✚ ✚ ✚

The idea now was to keep travelling with the town of Myponga always to the west of me. I jogged south, and it took some time before the simple knowledge surfaced that each dairy farm I ran through held milk. At the next farm-house, I crept into the milking shed and searched until I located the milk-vat. On the first gulped mouthful I almost gagged—pure cream! Stirring it up, I sipped down five 'cups' of delicious milk. Light rain had started to fall. A grain shed stood near the residence. Exhausted, I went there to take a healing catnap, hoping that before I again set out, the rain would have ended.

✚ ✚ ✚

A motorbike roaring by outside roused me from a plumbeous sleep. Tired and disoriented, I dropped down from the bags of grain and stumbled to the loading doors. The motorbike stopped at the house, about twenty or so metres from me. Part of the conversation I eavesdropped on in the misty rain slapped me in the face:

"What are those pigs doing on our front block?" Asked the pillion rider.

"How the fuck should I know!" Came the pungent retort. I didn't need to hear any more. I grabbed an empty grain sack and pelted away into the wet night, seeking height, knowing that their front block would be flat land. Somehow I had fallen back within the cordon's reach! As I gained height, I saw their questing torches fanned out behind me. The chase was on again—only this innings I might not be so lucky. I ran...

✚ ✚ ✚

One hour later... two farms had been crossed and a long hill negotiated. I halted to rest and to look back. The rain had ceased and the night-sky was clear. What I saw chilled my wits: five figures running in file using torches, less than a thousand paces behind me. In the vanguard were two tracker-dogs tugging on their long leads—and they obviously had my scent.

I bolted over the hilltop, reckless, and down the other side, oblivious to pitfalls: following a cow-path, to abruptly blunder into a creek! My floundering about in the icy water washed away all panic. I started to think. Stories I had read flashed to mind, of how the Indians always eluded the pursuing Bluecoats by riding along watercourses to break their trail.

Stumbling out of the creek—spurred by desperation—I pounded back up the cow-track, as hard as I could go; back up the hill towards the men and dogs I had fled from in a funk only minutes before. Almost at the top, my legs failing—winded and distraught—I veered off to my right perhaps twenty paces, then dropped down flat behind a boulder with only seconds to spare before two Alsatian dogs came bounding over the ridge.

I held my breath, lungs on fire. Both dog-handlers wore coveralls. Behind them laboured the other three. The flanking two wore quasi-military gear and each carried an Armalite rifle. The fifth one wore a policeman's uniform. My body cringed as they pounded past, only metres from me. One dog sensed the stratagem—for a moment it was over—but that handler kicked his dog on after the other one loping down the cow-path. I sucked oxygen into my starving lungs, willing my rigid body to relax while adjusting the grain bag over my body for cover. I watched from the boulder-strewn hillside.

At the creek, a tense discussion was going on. Torches flashed while the men worked the animals to confirm that my scent had ended at the water. I listened to them talk on their two-ways, rambling on, until finally they got an order: one dog and three men to go downstream, and the remainder to go upstream. What I'd hoped for—a senior man who read Westerns! I relaxed with more deep breathing to gather my strength.

**TORCHES
FLASHED
WHILE
THE MEN
WORKED
THE ANIMALS
TO CONFIRM
THAT MY
SCENT HAD
ENDED AT
THE WATER.**

I stayed hidden until both groups were well out of sight before crawling over the hill's crest. Filled with the joy of success, I strode away from there, headed north.

✛ ✛ ✛

Before sun-up, having visited two more dairies for milk, I settled in under a large shrub near a farm's driveway and gate. My legs stuck out, so I wrapped my feet and calves in the burlap-bag and lay back, relieved, drifting off to sleep as the sun gave notice of its dawning.

✛ ✛ ✛

A tractor chugging by woke me up. I felt quite safe where I lay in the filtered sunshine, so I drifted back into sleep; but again, I was disturbed. While trying to locate the tractor, the noise grew louder—menacing—and I feared for a moment that the tractor was bearing down on me and a small plane buzzed overhead!

Three things happened, inseparably linked: two nesting birds flew out of the bush; a family of rabbits scampered and disappeared; AND I jerked my burlapped feet in out of sight. The plane banked—it was turning back! Mastering myself, I pushed my unwilling legs back out.

Nothing else could have snared their attention! The aircraft's engine changed pitch as it dipped its nose, flying low over me. It then nosed up in the sky, banked, and again flew over me before resuming its original course. I breathed out a shaky sigh of relief.

It is only later one gets to ponder why we react the way we do under stress. Each of us is unique. Intuitively, I had relied on the few wild creatures to convince the plane-crew that I was not in the area. The roadblock and cowboy ploys played out earlier were also instinctive... based on experience. Whatever the reason, I refused to surrender to the clamouring animal-urge to change my hiding place. It was as much a risk to move, as it was to wait it out. My concerns gradually faded and sleep, surprisingly, returned.

+ + +

That night, when I set out for Adelaide, the sky was crystal clear so I had no problems navigating my way back to Meadows, then down to McClarenvale, to eventually walk to the plateau which overlooks the Reynella reservoir. A car-radio had earlier confirmed that the manhunt for me had intensified in the Myponga-Willunga region because I was, "still known to be contained in the closing dragnet."

The thickly grassed paddocks traversed and the numerous obstacles I'd encountered had weakened my resolve to not use a road (to avoid a 'confirmed sighting' of me) and so after twice being nearly caught in headlights, I sensibly searched out a squat to await the morning traffic when I would, hopefully, not seem so out of place. I had run and walked and plodded and crawled over forty kilometres of paddocks and back roads. I hadn't eaten solid food for four days. The pressures were finally taking their toll. Any exertion left me weak and panting.

I sat hidden in bushes halfway down the Reynella-hill road, using a comb I had found to tame my knotted hair and beard, while searching the bitumen for a safe vehicle to hitch a ride from. Soon the right car commenced its descent towards me. Clattering down the hill it raced, with no other vehicle in sight: an ancient beat-up Volkswagen. With bated breath, I stepped onto the road and stuck my thumb out. The candidate for a defect-sticker went flying past me— then groaned a protest of worn-out brakes. Almost around the next curve, it halted. I danced, triumphant, to the waiting ride.

A middle-aged woman drove and a mongoloid boy sat beside her. I said, "Thank you for stopping," as I scrambled into the back seat. And when the car got rolling, I ad-libbed, "I'm going into the city to lodge my dole-form;" sowing a false lead, just in case. "Are you going anywhere near there?"

"My son attends a special school," she explained. "I'll take you along South road as far as the tram-line, love. That should be a help to you."

All the while I talked with the woman, her son had stared at me swivel-necked. Concerned about my appearance, I sneaked a look in the rear-view mirror and saw why the boy couldn't take his eyes off me. I was dirty, scratched and bruised; my hair stuck out in wild disarray—I truly resembled a farmyard grotesque!

I could have kissed that kind old lady. I would NEVER have stopped for me the way I looked! Her act of charity warmed me. To return the trust, I relaxed into a rhythm of warm and friendly discussion with her and the boy. And when parting at the tramline I experienced a pang of loss, a sense of loneliness as they drove away, leaving me there.

VERY nervous and feeling exposed, I stood cross-armed at that tram-stop, while agonising over my appearance, wondering if the police would turn up before the tram to the beach arrived. Relieved, the tram won. No one seemed to be the least bit interested in my dishevelment as I stepped aboard (disturbing me even more)… until I got off at the Glenelg terminus where a few vagrant-types gawked at me from the jetty.

Entering the only milk-bar open, I bought myself a cold pie and pasty, and a big container of orange-juice. I was sick of milk!

+ + +

A short while later, sitting on the sand, slowly eating my first meal in five days, the soothing cadence of the waves calmed me. It was an extraordinary experience, and a delicious repast!

After basking in the morning sun, I had a cleansing wash in the sea, and rested until the trading shops opened for business.

I bought myself new underwear, jeans, a pull-over, socks and boots; then at the Life-savers' club, I luxuriated in a hot shower before changing into my new clothes and finally, at last, discarding the detested and smelly boob garb! Refreshed and confident, I strolled to the barbershop.

Later, I wandered along the sea front, shaved clean and sporting a crew cut, listening to the chatter of carefree children on their way to school. I deeply inhaled the crisp, salty tang of Freedom—like whisky on an empty stomach—while planning my next move, ever alert to the fact that my Sword of Damocles (capture) hovered one pace behind.

▼ Map detailing the path travelled after escaping

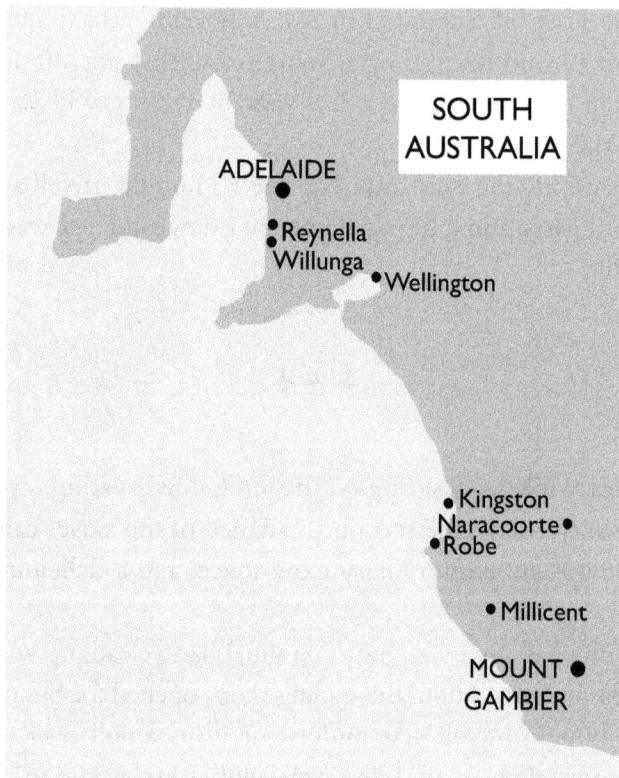

ARREST 2

DEFEAT THE FEAR OF DEATH

AND WELCOME THE DEATH OF FEAR

G. GORDON LIDDY

FEBRUARY 1979

ADELAIDE, S.A

Standing on the front lawn of my sister's house, watching her walk south with her children down the long street at Brahma Lodge, I saw two white sedan cars turn into view at the end of her street, 400 metres away. A premonition: they were coming for me. I even believe my sister, Rose, thought the same; she looked quickly back at me.

I could have bolted, though I didn't know if the reserves to get me away were there. I was so tired of it all. The many weeks of fox-and-hound raids, with the escalating pressures from the police, had finally caught up with me.

A newspaper had printed my open letter on December 13th, 1978, in which I publicly proclaimed my innocence and pleaded for an investigation. And I had made many phone-calls to report new facts to the media as they developed. My case had been stated. Now came the litmus test.

I remained motionless, keyed-up, watching the cars rapidly approach, sensing beyond doubt that they were police. It was safer if I were arrested outside the house; the reported antics of the detectives seeking me were enough to scare.

The racing cars kept piling on speed. For a fleeting moment foolish hope surged, then the tail car slammed on its brakes. The lead car flashed by, pulling to the right; two more vehicles zeroed in from other streets.

Nose down, the tail-car slid past me, screeching to a furious stop. The nearside rear door flew open and a bearded fat man, brandishing a short-barrelled shotgun, leapt out. A skinny man fell out behind him.

Crouched over with the gun at waist level, he forced his voice out in hoarse gusts of angry violence: "Run, Joe! I'm gunna blast you man if you don't! Run!"

I stayed unmoved. My sang-froid did not desert me. It was Sam the verballer, and he could easily kill—if given the justification. He knew that I had sought to have them both investigated by a tribunal. I had set in motion the final step of my surrender to ensure it; but somehow he must have gotten wind of my intention to use one of my sisters as an intermediary and, by arresting me before I could hand myself in, very adroitly pulled the rug out from under me.

Unfazed, I held both hands in sight, out from my body. Fatso ran over and struck me to the ground with the shotgun's butt. His intimidatory yell had failed to startle me into frightened activity—to be blasted down, "Trying to escape, Sir!"

Skinny handcuffed my wrists behind my back as I lay

face down, then disappeared into the house with the other police, except Fatso; he kept me prostrate on the lawn with the gun's muzzle pressed against my neck. I certainly wasn't going anywhere.

Reasonable calm soon prevailed after they satisfied themselves that no weapons were present. Within ten minutes I was being driven away in the rear of a police car, pressed under the feet of three backslapping detectives who quite boastfully told me that I'd have been 'wasted' had they surprised me inside the house. Being on the lawn had saved me, they said, thanks to witnesses.

HE KEPT ME PROSTRATE ON THE LAWN WITH THE GUN'S MUZZLE PRESSED AGAINST MY NECK.

+ + +

On arrival at Angus Street Police Headquarters, a photographer took my photo when going up the steps with Fatso. That picture later covered the entire front page of the evening Advertiser.

Inside the building, I spoke to the Inspector about how Fatso and Skinny had already planted evidence in my car and fabricated a confession for me. I asked Inspector H if this was going to be a repeat of that one. He stated that I'd be dealt with according to standard police rules.

He seemed genuinely disconcerted by my outspoken assertion and question. He said, "That doesn't occur with me in control." And, "whatever you choose to say will be recorded accurately, without anything 'added on' later." He then formally cautioned me in the presence of two others.

The offence of prison escape is usually established by documentation; a confession is not necessary to prove the link between the crime (actus rea) and the mind (mens rea) as it is for most criminal offences. I therefore knew that an interview in typed form would favour me and after some doubts were sorted out and Fatso sent out of the section... I agreed to be interviewed. Inspector H hovered in the background while it took place.

During the interview they charged me with escape from prison and illegal-use of a motor vehicle. They then took me to the Watch-house to be transported to Yatala prison's main security wing. I was the only remand prisoner in the entire complex of Yatala.

'I'll give myself up'

Escapee's offer

An escapee described by police as dangerous is offering to give himself up.

The man, Joseph Andrew Tog▊▊, 34, escaped from Mount Gambier Gaol on November 29 with another man, Werner ▊▊▊. ▊▊▊ was captured near Adelaide 10 days ago.

In a letter to "The Advertiser" posted in the city on Monday, Tog▊▊ says he is writing "to set a few facts straight, as the police have misadvised the public about me through you."

He offers to surrender in the presence of others on the condition he be allowed to remain silent because of alleged police harassment on his original arrest in September.

"I am not armed nor do I intend to be in the future. It is not my intent to resist apprehension with force; I will surrender peacefully," the letter says.

Senior police said yesterday they would accept Tog▊▊'s surrender under his terms.

Tog▊▊'s lawyer, Mr. M. A. Minarelli, after confirming the hand writing was Tog▊▊'s, said he would assist in any way he could.

Tog▊▊ has been linked by some commentators with members of the "Pub Gang" which netted more than $100,000 in ▊▊ breakings on hotels and clubs in SA's South-East and

Barossa Valley and the south-west of Victoria.

Both Tog▊▊ and ▊▊▊ were in the remand section of the Mount Gambier Gaol and were to appear before the South-Eastern District Criminal Court on charges relating to breakings in the area.

Tog▊▊ says in his letter he has not been charged with a hotel breaking offence.

"I am not a member of some Pub Gang of some notoriety," he says.

He says police are fabricating a case to support their earlier allegations that he was the perpetrator of "a number of certain types of crime."

"I sat virtually silent for three days, was assaulted, menaced, falsely charged and had a false record of interview conducted," he says.

He does not deny being in possession of property which police found.

"What I vigorously contest is my alleged admission of those crimes and how I came into possession of some of these articles and the wilful and malicious concocting of evidence by those two officers to further their own ends, whatever they might be."

He says police have not accounted for $30,800 cash which was in his

caravan at the time of his arrest. He claims incriminating evidence was put in his car.

He describes as "utter falsity" police charges that he assaulted two plainclothes police officers and attempted to escape.

"I was punched and kicked into submission — and did not fight back nor speak. The escape charge is to account for my wounds and any complaint I might utter."

He says he threw a typewriter to the floor while being questioned and claimed no interview took place.

He says he was falsely charged with assaulting two plainclothes police officers and with attempting to escape from their custody.

"So today falsely charged, I set out to obtain my freedom to allow me to bring my case before some jurisdiction of enquiry," he says.

"I will willingly surrender myself into the custody of a lawful agency ... with my rights to silence observed stringently — provided an independent and honest investigation into my allegations will take place involving this alleged Pub Gang that I am purported to be a member of."

Tog▊▊ was charged with breakings of three premises in Naracoorte. He was arrested at Elizabeth on September 6 in the company of a girl, 17, who is still in custody.

On the same day police made other arrests which they believed would break up a safe-cracking gang which preyed on country hotels, clubs and stores.

Tog▊▊ says in his letter he wants to help the 17-year-old girl involved in his case. He says she is

"totally innocent of any crime to my knowledge."

Tog▊▊ and ▊▊▊ escaped by carving a hole through a stone wall with a kitchen knife, climbing through a ceiling into a recreation yard, then up and over the prison wall using a tennis net.

Prison authorities said the two men had taken advantage of "many incomplete security precautions" in the gaol.

After the escape police described Tog▊▊ as "extremely dangerous" and said he had used a firearm to resist arrest in the past.

A special SA and Victorian police operation code-named Operation Fox resulted in five arrests after a month of intensive investigation into the hotel and club breakings.

● Contd. Page 7.

Joseph Andrew Tog▊▊

Part of Tog▊▊ letter to the Editor of "The Advertiser."

Many months of slogging fact-finding work followed, carried out by my able counsellor Mark M. Without his unstinting belief in me I don't ever doubt that those two criminal detectives would have succeeded in entombing me for a decade.

Between us, we were able to whittle down the bogus case against me, with Mark showing time and again—to impartial police and the courts—that each allegation lacked substance. They plummeted from sixteen, to twelve, to four, to one. One!

Out of 16 allegations made during and after my original arrest at Elizabeth, only a single offence remained to be answered: money suspected of being unlawfully obtained. The only charge which had any valid basis. I gambled daily.

Three charges of receiving (suspected) stolen-property were later preferred—it was the property given to me by Fritz. There were eleven months of anguish between my arrest in September at Elizabeth with Diane, and subsequent hearing in August the following year.

✦ ✦ ✦

In the Dock at the Adelaide Sittings, I pleaded guilty to Receiving, Escape from Prison and Illegal-use. A plea, composed and written by me, detailing all events leading up to my court appearance, (which became part of the draft for this story) was submitted to Judge B who at the hearing's finish, stated that he accepted my argument for mitigation. He then passed sentence on me.

Receiving—two years.

Illegal-use—six months.

Escape—two months concurrent. In effect, nothing except the recording of the conviction. An unheard of penalty for prison escape!

Judge B went on to say, among other germane comments, that some of the detectives in my case had a lot to answer for.

✚ ✚ ✚

A few weeks later at the Adelaide Magistrates Court, waiting in a cell for my 'money offence' to begin, Fatso and Co. barged in to strike a bargain. The gist of their 'offer' was that I discontinue my outcry against them and to plead guilty that day to the money charge—and if I didn't grasp the logic of their argument, they warned, more offences would be preferred.

They had me on the canvas, but to quote James J Corbett, "The man who can get up and fight one more round is never beaten." So I argued on for a better deal, not expecting to win; but when they consented to not provide the court with an antecedent-sheet of my criminal history, I felt happier as though I had won that round.

In the courtroom, the Police Prosecutor spoke quietly with me about my change of plea until the Magistrate made his appearance; and the court began. The charge, 'found in possession of money suspected of being stolen or unlawfully obtained', was read aloud and my plea was asked for.

I sipped a shallow breath, then said, "I'm guilty, Your

Worship," trying to still my heart's flutter. The die cast.

The Magistrate asked the Prosecutor, "Any prior criminal history on this man?"

The Prosecutor, shuffling his feet, replied, "None in South Australia, Your Worship."

The Magistrate's penetrating eyes bored

▲ Joe, South Channel Fort, 1989

right into me as he studied my face. Without averting his eyes from mine he directed his next question to the Prosecutor. "Does he have an Interstate history sheet?"

"It hasn't been brought to my attention if he has, sir," replied the Prosecutor, riffling through his miscellany of papers to cover his nerves.

I did not move, nor change my expression. Without a doubt this astute Magistrate knew I had 'previous form', and suspected something was being put over him.

After a minute of silence, the Magistrate purred, "Well, I can wait. You have twenty minutes to find out." And strode from the courtroom.

The court's duty-cop escorted me to a small waiting room where the Prosecutor and I had a hasty conversation. He declared, "I will have to submit your form sheet now. I tried to help you but I daren't go any further." And he turned to leave.

"Wait!" I demanded. "The detectives made a deal with me and so did you." I went on to explain; "My plea of guilty is to save you and the police a protracted prosecution. If you declare my record, I'll get extra time for certain!" I tried to keep calm.

"But it's gone beyond what I anticipated!"

"All you need say," I impressed, "is that you have no sheet. If they haven't provided you with one then it isn't your fault is it?" I could see that he was wavering. "Two grand of that money's legit—only the rest is in dispute." I then added a hollow threat: "If you don't go through with it, I'll withdraw my plea and expose the deal!"

His face was a video of indecision: "I will need to speak with the detectives."

✚ ✚ ✚

Fifteen minutes later we were back in the courtroom. The Magistrate imperiously asked of the prosecutor, "Have you been able to locate a record?"

The Prosecutor calmly replied, "There doesn't appear to be a criminal history interstate, Your Worship," looking relaxed behind the bar-table. "I have been assured by the detectives in this case that their search during the recess has revealed nothing of substance."

My tensed muscles relaxed. Pleased, I listened to him expand on the subject; to explain how I was currently serving a prison term with a nexus to the money and he was therefore not asking for an additional term of imprisonment.

The Magistrate heard him out, and then wrote for a

lengthy time in the court's ledger. When finished, he lifted his head to address me. "My original intention was to sentence you to eighteen months," he coldly stated. "But I have been dissuaded from that course. According to the Prosecutor's source, you have no previous convictions."

At this point the Magistrate turned his piercing stare onto the two verballers sitting impassive at the courtroom's rear. His gaze returned to pin me. "The law has been broken and YOU will be punished for it. I am therefore imposing a prison term of twelve months." He glared at me. "It is to be served cumulative." He rose from behind the bench and stalked out of my life.

So ended another day in court.

FLIGHT

THE ROAD OF EXCESS CAN LEAD (SOMETIMES) TO THE PALACE OF WISDOM

WILLIAM BLAKE

SUNDAY 29TH JUNE 1980
ADELAIDE, S.A

Breakfast time, and already the airport was a buzz of activity, making me squirm and think that everyone was staring at me as I drove past them towards the parking area. My beard had been shaved off, leaving a zapata-moustache, and I wore gold-rim glasses. I had darkened my hair and combed a tint of grey through it. The pants I wore were a bit baggy but the thick jacket was a perfect fit. The bag on the back seat had provided everything; even a Victorian drivers-license. And six hundred dollars. Yet still I was tense, ready for the cry of, "There he is!" And my stomach bred millions of moths.

I found a place to park and got out. I was confused about what to do with the keys at first, but then I realised that they were expendable copies. I grabbed the bag and locked the doors before hobbling away. My feet throbbed from stone bruises, and the tight shoes I wore didn't help. A pair of sneakers is a must, I thought, as I headed for the taxi rank.

+ + +

My mind would only function in the present and it was difficult to plan ahead as every event loomed out of sync. Sensory overload—like the time a 'friend' once slipped me an L.S.D. tab. The shock of being plucked from prison and let loose in mega-society had spun me out.

Sitting in the rear of the taxi on the way to Adelaide's central railway station, I willed myself to review the plan I had cobbled together the night before. (Due to the anxiety I experienced after the prison-break, the safe-house address told to me had slipped my mind; and no amount of brow furrowing could recall it!)

Three phone-calls were made. The first call was a local one to have a friend assure Diane that all was well and not to expect me. (Our relationship had ended.) The second call was long-distance and two-fold: to attempt a link-up with Fritz and to get some personal property taken to a pick-up place before the shit hit the fan. Knowing police and their tactics, I knew that my disappearance would be used as an excuse by them to enter homes and hassle people who had no real connection to me. That's normal.

I also planned to avoid the conditioned reflex of running straight for known territory, by sitting it out in the hunter's den. Then when the frenzy of door bashing abated, I'd travel to Victoria. In the meantime, the third phone-call, to a friend in Melbourne, was to start the gathering of money from friends who were sympathetic to my plight. A 'help-Joe-to-survive-fund' you could call it, now that I had to make it alone.

Near the station on the way to Victoria Square, I bought sneakers, thick socks, a pullover and a blanket, a sheath knife and a few other articles necessary for camping out. I already had a torch and a transistor in the bag.

Victoria Square is where the tramline to Glenelg in the west begins and the bus service from Aldgate in the east ends. My intention was to eventually use both; first to the seaside and later to the hills.

▲ Victoria Square, Adelaide, September 1998

The tram was the best transport I could have chosen. Its therapeutic swaying as it sped from stop to stop eased the tension in my body; gradually my thoughts began to gel for the first time. I knew that the pressure of being hunted is mostly self-induced and if I allowed the hunter's tactics to roil my thinking I could easily become desperate. The best way for me to avoid contemplating the reality was to think of it as a game of chase, with no penalty other than re-imprisonment when recaptured.

At the Glenelg end of the tramline, I bought food and drink before setting out along the Esplanade. I strolled the beach, going south, listening to the waves tell their story of peace. With the bag over one shoulder and a towel over the other, I wandered along, taking in all that was happening around me; and the only people I saw were a few kids on bikes and a housewife or two outside, pottering in their front gardens. The tranquillity of the walk made it hard for me to believe that I was, at the time, the most sought after person in South Australia. The time: about 10:00 am.

+ + +

A few hours later, I stood beneath the sloping hills of Seacliff. I took a swim, and then used the nearby caravan park shower before entering the Seacliff hotel for a counter-lunch and beer. It was my intention not to listen to any of the news bulletins because they tend to influence my actions; however, one bulletin was forced upon me by the television—blasting the tranquillity out of me as well as my appetite. Newsflash! Dangerous escapee flees prison!

The food lost its flavour and instead of lingering over it, as I wanted to, I hastily downed my drink and left the hotel. It, again, felt like everyone was staring at me! I fled to the deserted sea front.

I sat on the sand, drowning my thoughts with the transistor, until rain sent me back, seeking cover, to the small group of shops next to the hotel. I rummaged through the displayed wares of a second-hand store to find a cap and overcoat: then it was up the hill, across the train-line and down Brighton road, heading back towards the city.

▲ Brighton/Seacliff Beach and the Esplanade Hotel, Adelaide, late September 1998

The round trek had accomplished three main objectives: settled my mind, passed the day, and released my pent-up energy. By the time I arrived back at Victoria Square I'd be ready to head for Sterling, a town about 20 kilometres to the east, nestled in the Mount Lofty Ranges—the second leg of my plan.

+ + +

The bus laboured its way up the winding hill road with me in the half-empty rear trying to look inconspicuous behind a newspaper, but feeling naked and exposed. I knew that whatever happened, I had to appear normal and, at all times, to move as though I had a destination in mind. The unusual is what always attracts attention.

The first town the bus reached lacked what I sought, so I sat there worrying that if the next few stops were unfruitful too then I'd be forced to go into Stirling. The detective contingent stationed there had a bad reputation and they were sure to have been briefed, as Stirling straddled the highway to Melbourne; the route most likely traversed when fleeing the state. I recognised the risk, but I knew of no other way that had the same balance of fulfilling my need and wasting two days in virtual safety.

The bus slowed to a halt. Nervously hefting my bag, I stood with the few passengers alighting in this hamlet. I felt excitement, while simultaneously fearing further exposure when off the bus; but this place had what I hoped for—a station and, therefore, a train-line.

Stepping down like I knew the town, I paced quickly back the way the bus had come, paralleling the 'line out of town until an embankment hid me from view. I scrambled up the embankment, out of sight.

I crouched there for a while, watching the road below, before gradually wending my way deeper into the trees to get to the railway line.

Dropping down to the stone ballast, I placed my ear to a rail to detect if a train was coming. Satisfied that it was safe, I headed for the setting sun, back towards Adelaide. If spotted, it was

IF SPOTTED, IT WAS UNLIKELY THAT I WOULD BE SUSPECTED OF BEING THE 'DANGEROUS' PRISON ESCAPEE unlikely that I would be suspected of being the 'dangerous' prison escapee—a fleeing man would head *out of* Adelaide.

In less than a kilometre, I reached a natural clearing suitable to make a camp. I gathered wood for a fire and constructed a crude lean-to as a rain and wind break. Then the sun set, blanketing the region in darkness, except for where I sat rugged up and warm next to my cosy camp-fire. I was at peace, not worried about tomorrow, though I wondered what fate would hold in store for me when I descended to the enmity of Adelaide. I fell asleep to the soft music of falling rain.

✛ ✛ ✛

MONDAY 30TH JUNE 1980
ADELAIDE, S.A

I awoke, knowing that things were not right. I could sense it. Yet the sun was up and birds chirped out a cacophony of sound. I snatched up the transistor to slip it in my pocket... and the anxiety faded; its switch was still on, and no sound came forth! The batteries were dead flat.

It had nagged me all the way up in the bus: extra batteries—a simple requirement to overlook, which I had, and could not remedy. If the hunt were to enter the hills now, I'd have no means of knowing until they fell on me in force. Not being sighted by anyone was now imperative.

While moving about preparing a meagre breakfast, I discovered muscles that I never knew I owned! Aching all over, my feet were so swollen at first I couldn't pull on my sneakers. Soaking both feet in an icy rivulet further down the train-track improved their circulation, and helped me to think.

At least two days had to pass before I tried for Melbourne, and even then the risk was barely acceptable. It would be a fortnight or more before the South Australian and Victorian police scaled down their joint operations in relation to me. If the quarry remains unflushed for two weeks they gradually return to the less exciting investigative methods. But I couldn't afford to wait that long. I knew that the audacity of the prison break-in would be interpreted—particularly by the police—as a slap in the face of authority. And bearing in mind that it would be declared a major-crime, I planned not to be back in Adelaide before Tuesday, when the thrust of the local search would have lost its impetus.

+ + +

The trek down was the most free, most idyllic, period of my time at large. I revelled in the rebirth of my body and the return of my quintessential self; nature's way of voiding the venom insinuated into my mind by prison regime. Each kilometre revealed new insights as I crossed water, slid down slopes and ventured through tunnels. It forced me to again confront the facts of my predicament, this time without the impingement of fear to influence my mind and cloud my reasoning. I decided that I would try to conduct myself as if I were a free man (except for basic precautions) and not as a hunted man. The quality of my freedom meant more to me than the quantity of it.

Moves to tighten security follow bold escape

Electronic surveillance equipment may be installed at Yatala Labor Prison following the daring escape of a maximum-security prisoner early on Saturday.

Joseph—Andrew Tognolini

The Chief Secretary, Mr Radda, said the escape of Joseph Andrew Tognolini, and other recent escapes from Yatala, highlighted the need for more surveillance in the gaol.

Mr. Radda said a feasibility study of installing the surveillance equipment in Yatala had been put before the director of the Correctional Services Department, Mr. W. A. Stewart, on Friday and was being considered.

A police spokesman said Tognolini escaped from a maximum-security cell in the maximum security section of the gaol by cutting the bars on his window with oxy-acetylene equipment.

A gate also was cut with the equipment. Police said accomplices drove into Yatala to free Tognolini.

He was serving four years for breaking offences.

The Premier, Mr. Tonkin, has ordered an immediate enquiry into the escape.

Mr. Radda said a departmental enquiry had begun shortly after the news of the escape and he expected the result late next week.

Mr. Radda yesterday visited Yatala and saw where the escape took place.

The State Parliamentary Leader of the Australian Democrats yesterday called for the resignation of Mr. Radda.

Mr. Millhouse said any enquiry into the escape and security at Yatala should be "full and open to the public."

Mr Millhouse said that unless Mr. Radda could give an honest assurance that there would be no further escapes of the kind at the weekend he should resign.

He said that with all the recent escapes in SA any enquiry might have to be broadened to include all of SA's gaol system.

"Gates were enough to do putting them into prison in the first place without having to chase escaped," he said.

Mr Millhouse said he had heard reports that there had been only "one or two" guards on duty in the section where Tognolini escaped.

Mr Stewart said the normal number of staff had been on duty at the gaol.

Tognolini was a member of the "pub gang" which stole more than $100,000 in 40 breakings on hotels and clubs in the south-east of SA and in south west Victoria.

Tognolini and another member of the gang, Werner Roman, escaped from Mount Gambier Gaol in November, 1979, by digging through a wall.

Roman was recaptured the following month but escaped again last November and is still free.

Tognolini, 30, is described as 198 centimetres (6 ft. 5 in.), with brown hair and brown eyes.

At the time of the escape he had a full beard.

He is considered dangerous and has to the past used firearms to resist arrest.

The escape has been declared a single crime and is being investigated by the special crime squad led by Detective Chief Inspector S. Pawelski.

Police have asked anyone with information to contact the crime intelligence unit on 217 6133.

Being sought after for escape was bad enough so I had no wont to add to the problem, though it was inevitable that I would, out of necessity, break the law in a few minor areas such as false papers, turning a blind eye, and doing things which were not quite legal. But I resolved nothing serious, even if it meant the loss of my freedom.

Having made that decision, going underground in Melbourne was no longer as imperative as I had thought it to be. It would now be only a staging ground for Queensland. And Fritz, after escaping from Yatala had already eluded arrest for six months, was not necessary to my plan of sun, sand and real freedom. Someday I must again take that same restorative descent.

+ + +

TUESDAY 1ST JULY 1980
ADELAIDE, S.A

8:30 pm: cold and windy. I shivered in a park near a schoolyard, hunched in shadow beside a bush, waiting to place a phone-call. One had already been made with good results

and this one would determine whether or not I had transport to Melbourne, 700 kilometres away.

If prison was the only consequence of my re-capture
then it wouldn't have driven me so, but being in the grip
again of those two verballers did! The fear started gnawing...
I went and made the second call.

✦ ✦ ✦

I was to leave that night! Harry, an old buddy who idealised
friendship, promised that a car would be at the Brighton-
jetty in two hours. I danced a jig on the way back to a mate's
flat where earlier I'd freshened up and laundered my clothes.
Bob was still there and he steadfastly refused to listen to reason when I explained that travelling alone to the pick-up
point was wiser for me and safer for him.

He prevailed and so we set out on foot—it wasn't far to
go—using avenues and back streets rather than hazarding the
main roads. The seriousness of our jaunt didn't deter us from
laughing at each other's jokes until, I'm sure we resembled
two larrikin school boys on the wag—almost ending my run
that night!

When entering the street we walked, the headlights of
a vehicle lit us up as it came in off the main road eighty-or-
so metres behind. Caught by surprise, we glanced over our
shoulders guiltily—a blue-dome! Our instincts took control
(a bad reflex to allow) with Bob bounding ahead in fright
and me less than a pace behind in full stride.

The engine of the police-van roared in response—not
knowing why we bolted but never-the-less taking up the

chase—and its headlights swelled to high beam, spotlighting us on the roadway like rabbits. Skidding to an abrupt halt, I turned and faced them.

If caught with me, Bob would go to prison. But if I were recognised they might forget about him in their haste to nab me. So dropping the bag, I sped back and across the street to a side street, fully revealed in the blazing lights. And the van swerved to block my path.

It missed me! The divvy came to a shuddering stop in the north side gutter of the side street. I vaulted over the front fence of the second house on the south side. My pulse hammered. I pounded down the far side of the house, to swing across the back yard, past a startled dog and over the side fence into the driveway of the corner house.

A second dog—luckily quite small—attacked my ankles, berserk, as I scurried to the front gate. The first dog, caught off guard by my flashing pace, made up for its tardiness by attacking the two intruders pursuing me through its domain.

The divisional-van sat empty, its lights on and its doors agape. Pelting across, I retrieved my bag and, as house lights came on and dogs all round barked hysterically, I raced away down the street searching for Bob. Lungs on fire, my senses ultra-alert, I never laid eyes on him all the way to the pick-up point.

A SET-UP MY MIND SCREAMED AS THE BEARDED FACE STARED OUT AT ME.

✛ ✛ ✛

Standing in shadow and hidden from view, I studied the jetty's parking area. Two cars were angle-parked facing the sea wall, each with a person sitting in front and two more cars, empty, stood opposite, parallel to the Esplanade Hotel. Which one?

I watched and waited… until by lights of passing cars, I knew. A slim person sat in the nearer car. And in the car furtherest away, a big man hunched behind the steering wheel. Harry is a large man and when he said he would deliver, he must have meant it literally, I thought.

Waiting until after a motorbike roared past, with no other lights in sight, I crossed the esplanade to the beachside footpath and hurried towards the safety of Harry's car. Striding past the first car I peered in—a young woman—and my eyes swept on to the next car with Harry resting over the steering wheel.

"Joe!" Came a startled cry, pitched high, "it's this car!" The passenger door of the car I'd just passed swung open.

I stumbled to a halt, turning to stare back in surprise at the woman.

And the man raised his head, causing me to look at him. A set-up! A set-up my mind screamed as the bearded face stared out at me. I would have bolted from there, but fright rooted me to the footpath. I glared at the man instead.

But it wasn't Sam, the verballer. Except for the beard, it looked nothing like him! Trembling in nervous reaction, I slumped onto the seat beside the attractive woman, an apparent stranger, wondering how she had known me.

"Yes it is cold, isn't it?" She observed, misinterpreting my shaking hands as an indication of the weather. "The heater will soon warm you up though!" She cheerily stated.

Rather than disillusion her view, I simply asked, "Where's Harry? Why did he send you?"

"My pop's a good friend of his," she explained. "They thought it'd be better if I took you, Joe." She offered her hand and said, "My name's Camellia. Do you remember me?" We shook hands as I studied her.

Her name had triggered off the memory of a woman I had met a few times with Harry's daughter. It's amazing what make-up can do to change a person. Obviously my appearance hadn't changed much: which said a lot for my attempt at disguise!

I enquired, "Have you made arrangements to get yourself home, or will you need a taxi?"

"Joe, these wheels are mine," she stated, laughter in her voice. "No one gets to drive them; not even my dad! So you're stuck with me as chauffer."

Her suppressed excitement and presence of only a few minutes had already worked its alchemy, but I had to ask: "Have you considered the risk you're taking, Cam? Are you certain it's what you want to do?"

Cam's answer was to start the engine and reverse out, and then zoom up Jetty road. She quipped, "Well, I'm yours to command! Which way do we go; inland or the coast?" Her friendly personality had me captivated and at ease. I threw my bag onto the rear seat, relaxed, trusting myself to Cam.

We set out together, her happy and me not so lonely, along Brighton road, up the long hill to South road and on to Meadows, for Wellington and the ferry.

The meandering coastal drive to Melbourne developed into a memorable one for me that would be unfair to elaborate on. But I will say that we grew to know each other quite well. We parted with mutual regret and respect.

+ + +

Being an offspring of Melbourne, it was inevitable that anywhere I went I risked encountering people who knew me. And I did. But it surprised and gladdened me the amount of times aid was spontaneously offered, without encumbrance, once they heard the facts. I should not have been as surprised as I was with their ready charity. An Aussie characteristic is to side with the underdog.

And remarks at the time convinced me that helping satisfied their need to rebel. They saw me as one to be admired and not 'dobbed in'. Stems from the convict days, no doubt.

Unfortunate, there were a few social misfits (to interpose a fact of life) who hoped that I'd play havoc with society—an instrument of their own bitterness. They offered me weapons, tools and lurks to do. I accepted all things that were convertible to cash and all else I declined.

+ + +

FRIDAY 4TH JULY 1980
MELBOURNE, VICTORIA

It seemed that Fritz and I would be meeting after all. The second call on my first night out had caught up with him and my belated message had been passed on. In response, Fritz had contacted a relative of mine to say that he was on his way to Victoria: he'd left a phone-number in code (a simple system transposing my sister's name for numbers) which I rang that day.

AFTER HE HANDED ME $500 SAYING THAT IT WAS A GIFT, I STUDIED THE PILE FOR COUNTERFEITS!

The answering woman said that she expected Fritz to be there for dinner and would pass on any message I cared to leave. So I gave her a similarly encoded number for him.

That night Fritz rang to confirm a meet and, at 8:30 pm we gripped hands in Livingstone Street, Preston, not far from the College of Crime. We drove to the local caravan-park to prop and talk in relative safety. The camper-van he drove had virtually every convenience fitted—including a sink, toilet and fridge—so in comfort we lazed, sipping beer, recounting in turn the events surrounding us during the past hectic week.

Having more to say, Fritz related what he had done since he'd escaped from Yatala prison... and then I told of how I had been 'released' (if I may call it that) and how I got myself to Melbourne.

▲ Pentridge prison

The day after my prison-break, Fritz said he was on the last leg of a round trip from Sydney to Adelaide and back. The police-scramble to snare me had almost netted him (like his arrest at the farmhouse), only this time the New South Wales hinterland was less than a swift hour's drive ahead of him. He went to ground as though HE were the hunted one instead of me!

Fritz followed the media's growing coverage of my escape while he camped at Narrabri, and after hearing of the furore he informed Sydney to offer aid if requested. Then came my contact number. The rest fell into place.

It would not be unfair to label Fritz a Zurich-gnome; so when he pulled a wad of money from his wallet, I was somewhat taken aback because it looked as if he was going to lay it on me. After he handed me $500 saying that it was a gift, I studied the pile for counterfeits!

Anyhow, he soon agreed with me that sunny Queensland was the best choice and if I didn't mind his company, we could travel north together in his van. I agreed with Fritz because he must have been doing something right to elude capture for so long!

+ + +

The weekend stretched ahead of us, with ample time to complete what we wanted to do before leaving on Monday. Fritz dropped me off in the city where I later met a person who imparted some very disturbing news.

What isn't commonly known, though often applied, is the custom of police using criminals to flush out criminals. Good in theory, but flawed in practice. Once the leash is slipped they lose control of their dog—and dogs some of them are! Many an unmarked grave exists to stand testimony that a crime is not a crime if it goes uninvestigated. Ask anyone in the know!

The inside of Pentridge prison held the best and worst of Melbourne's underworld and it was from there that the warning came to me about two men from Sydney, methodically seeking my whereabouts. The rumour (spread by police) was that I still had diamonds from before my arrest in Adelaide… and that I sought a passport to flee the country.

I had the sum total of $1,800 to my name, an amount barely able to get me to Brisbane in safety. And to state the obvious, why should I flee the only developed nation with the customary cries of, "She'll be sweet, mate!" and "Have another beer?" The sunshine state shone brighter by the hour. I slept lightly that night.

+ + +

SATURDAY 5TH JULY 1980
MELBOURNE, VIC

My experiences have taught me to use public transport wherever practical, but an evening meeting had been pre-arranged on my behalf by someone who thought, like most, that an isolated site is preferable to a crowded one when on the run. (Crowds and inner suburbs are always safer.) Anyway, the hotel where I was to meet the collector of my 'help Joe' fund was in an outer suburb.

By removing both number plates of a car borrowed and then replacing its rear one with a pilfered front plate, I protected the lender. The drive was slow and careful without a cop-car sighted until, wheeling into the hotel's side street, a divisional-van stopped to give me the right of way. It surprised me that my pounding heart didn't get me arrested on suspicion; it beat so loudly! My composure upset, I parked there until I settled, before venturing out of the car.

+ + +

Light rain fell as I hurried to the hotel's entrance, into the public bar and through to the lounge at the rear. I bought a whiskey before strolling over to where two women sat alone at a table, to casually enquire if they minded me sitting there.

The taller one snapped, "Find your own seat!" which her plump companion countered by saying, "No; I don't mind." She smiled at me. "Please sit down."

So I sat and talked nonsense until the tall one's bladder urged her to the toilet. I hugged and quickly kissed my friend before palming from her a thick manila envelope held ready. In a rush of words we talked, till her companion (a stranger to me) returned to defend Pamela from what she perceived as a pick-up attempt. I bought another round of drinks; then eased out of their company into the night.

I felt good walking out of the pub. Inside me the two whiskeys sat well. Warm and relaxed, I inhaled the cool night air. The car waited in a side street to my left and I walked casually towards it thinking about which route to take while cars flashed by, their tyres swishing and headlights ablaze.

At the corner I gazed around at the few pedestrians like myself, surreptitiously confirming that all was well; then I headed for my car parked eight vehicles down. The money-filled envelope in my pocket made me wonder if I'd been wise in taking a rain-check on Pam's offer of staying at her place for the night.

A shadow of movement triggered a reflex. Instinctively, I ducked whatever it was hurtling straight at my head, dodging aside in fright—but not quickly enough! A blow struck my shoulder, smashing me to the pavement. Twisting in the dark, I squirmed away from the looming man-shape above me, only to be punched from behind. There were two of them.

Side kicking, I tried to sweep out the feet from under the one in front, but he jumped nimbly over my leg—with a large revolver in his fist! He scythed it down at me, caught by surprise, to strike me a stunning head blow. Pain washed my forehead; blood trickled down.

The one behind grabbed my hair and chin, forcing me to the concrete. Fingers splayed out, I stabbed upwards striking his face—then clawed downwards, hard, feeling skin tear.

"You friggen animal!" He cried out in pain, and punched a numbing blow to the base of my skull. I was stunned, and he dragged me easily back, supine, to the bloodied wet path. My life was in jeopardy.

In panic, I lashed out in rapid succession at the gunman—shin and groin—but before collapsing he struck me a crippling blow, with his revolver to my chest. A wave of nausea caught me. I was finished, almost. Grunting in pain, the gunman tried to barrel-whip my face. I lashed out wildly with hands and feet, writhing in the other attacker's strangling grip.

But my twisting turns allowed the gunsel to dive in on my left side. He gripped my forearm, hammering my pinioned hand with his steel-filled right… until I felt a bone crack. The next blow was agony!

Ready to give in to them, I heard an exclamation of shock nearby. In desperation—a wild surge of hope—I pleaded, "Help me! Please help me, somebody!"

An instant response came from the main road. "Hey! You there!" a man's stern voice demanded. "Leave him alone!"

The gun-wielder stopped and turned to threaten the

speaker. "Piss off you turd," he snarled, "or you'll get the same." He actually turned back and struck me again!

"Hurry up, mates. Trouble!" My saviour's voice shouted, "Call the cops!" And he pounded to my aid.

The gunny on his knees defiantly spat back, "Get away from here. We are the police. If you –" My Samaritan kneed him in the head.

Screaming in pain, he landed in the gutter. Then raised his gun. The fight resumed as I lunged for the weapon to lock the cylinder—with different odds now!

Two more men rushed into the affray. I struggled out from under them all, wresting the gun free of my attacker's grip. I struck him a savage blow in retaliation for ambushing me. And again I struck him with the gun!

There were wild obscenities and a din of sound all round—the slap of more heavy feet approaching—I staggered away, gasping, trembling from exertion. My hand pulsed pain, pain.

In the car, anxious to flee, I fumbled out the keys and started the motor. Without a glance back, I sped out of the area towards the city skyline. And as the kilometres grew my fears abated, and thought resumed.

A place to park and clean my wounds was a must. I would like to have thanked my rescuers but, if the two drygulchers really were police, I'd be jumping out of the fry pan and into the fire.

I STRUCK HIM A SAVAGE BLOW IN RETALIATION FOR AMBUSHING ME

+ + +

At the end of a dirt road, near a small creek, I soaked my torn shirt and used it to bathe the lacerations until I was satisfied that the bleeding had stopped. My lips and cheekbone were stinging, but the real pain pulsed from a deep gash on top of my head. My hand hurt only if I tried to use it: so I sat there soaking it in the cold water, thinking about what had nearly happened. The conclusions were not the kind I liked entertaining.

In the car I studied the revolver, hoping that my reasoning was flawed. But it wasn't. The weapon was a five-shot 45 Bulldog with its serial number filed off—not a type the police would use, unless they intended to plant it on me.

Either Pam's offer was to lure me back to her house to be captured, or the one who arranged the meeting set me up. Rather than condemn without proof, I allowed them both the benefit of a Winston Churchill quote: Loose lips sink battleships. But no way would I venture near those two again!

The abduction attempt frightened me more than I cared to admit. I clutched the Bulldog between my thighs like a talisman during the thoughtful drive back to the city. From now on, no more arranged meetings, nor returning to any place after leaving it!

Pam's envelope held twelve hundred dollars. Adding that to what I already had, raised my total cash to four thousand seven hundred and I still had all Sunday to canvass!

I didn't sleep too well that night.

+ + +

TELEX 5(Sat) 7(July) 1980 Qld.

BUNDABERG. Break and enter of Hardware
store... safe cut... money and property stolen.
BUNDABERG. Break and enter of Sawmill...
safe cut... money stolen.

+ + +

SUNDAY 6TH JULY 1980
MELBOURNE, VIC

Except for a variety of aches and pains, my appearance was
not too bad considering the thrashing I had suffered. The
cuts were covered with band-aids and my hand was taped
up tight. I'd shaved the front of my head to appear older and
wore John Lennon glasses to replace the pair lost in the fight.
My nondescript clothing was nothing to envy nor attract
attention. I compiled a list of five people to visit that day
and this time I carried some insurance—I took along the
Bulldog.

The train system in Melbourne is, in my opinion, the
best in Australia. I travelled back and forth all day, never
once spotting a hostile or anyone exuding that arrogant
confidence displayed by detectives and real criminals. By the
afternoon my cash had risen by another twelve hundred—
almost six thou in hand!

That evening I went to visit the manageress of a massage parlour (one of the few who really did grind at that trade for her children's sake) who is second to none when it comes to gleaning information. I needed to know more about my attackers.

The news Kat imparted was pleasant to hear. Only one was seeking me now and he had made the mistake of threatening people. Also it gratified me to learn that the other one had been hurt seriously enough to be hospitalised. She promised to seek more information for me.

While helping to close-up the premises, Kat hinted at a freebie massage (a service I really needed) but the kind she meant was solely genital and unfortunately would only aggravate my aching body! Sadly, I had to decline. And the money she offered me was out of the question.

I bid Kat goodbye at the train-station and after she'd driven away, I hurried back to the parlour to climb in through a window I had left unlatched. I soaked in a hot bath first; cooked dinner; then settled myself comfortably on the lounge. Within minutes, I was asleep.

✚ ✚ ✚

TELEX 6(Sun) 7(July) 1980
Qld.

BUNDABERG.
Break and enter
of Hotel… safe cut…
$7000 stolen.

Monday 7th July 1980
Melbourne, Vic

There was no cause for haste when I awoke—the agreed time to meet Fritz was 11:00 am—so I ate a leisurely breakfast, showered and trimmed the moustache before writing Kat a thank-you note, explaining the raided fridge and placing it under the teapot.

I headed for Preston full of jauntiness, not knowing that a simple act of escape would stir the Authorities more than rape, armed robbery, or even murder. It's true that a slap across the face will oft-times trigger a harsher response than a kick to the groin. Machiavelli made observations in The Prince germane to that subject.

"Your case has been declared a major-crime," were Fritz's very disheartening first words on entering his van. "They've posted a large reward and will not stop the hunt for you now."

Momentarily, a cold finger of hopelessness touched me, mentally dashed by the importance of what remained unsaid. I sat listening to him elaborate, detailing why we must make our way separately to Queensland. The risk to him of being captured with me was far too high, he said. And we had to make other arrangements. I agreed, asking him to contribute.

Fritz unfolded army survey-maps of the eastern states—duplicates of which he later gave

THE RISK TO HIM OF BEING CAPTURED WITH ME WAS FAR TOO HIGH

me—and together we conned out a few tentative routes, while pooling our joint knowledge of the North. We agreed eventually that Bowen, north of Mackay, was an ideal place to re-meet.

He would travel fast via Sydney while I proceeded at my own pace, both expecting to reach there before Saturday 12th. Our contact was to be through a mutual associate: Fritz was to phone-in each morning and I at night. A missed call twice in a row would signal that the other was again alone.

While Fritz showered in preparation to leaving, I racked my brain for transport: train, bus, car, or even a small plane—but none were safe. A truck from depot to depot was a possibility… and then I remembered Coz.

A hasty trip to the phone-box confirmed that he wasn't in the book. I knew he lived a long way out and rather than travel so far on speculation I rang the local library, explaining to the lady that I needed some names out of the McDougal directory. I gave her the suburb and road, plus Coz's surname, to ascertain if he lived there still and if so, the names of a few of his neighbours nearby. She suggested that I call back in an hour.

Fritz delivered me to the Coburg train-station and before buying a ticket, I returned the librarian's call. The names she relayed were what I wanted: two of them were listed in the phone book. The first number was answered by a crotchety woman who listened to half of what I had to say—then hung up on me! But the second number elicited a speedy response from a young girl who told me, "Coz is home 'cause his truck is broke."

I asked her to tell him to pick me up at the train-station after three o'clock, explaining to her that if I gave my name

▲ Joe at South Channel Fort, Port Phillip Bay, 1988

it would spoil the surprise. To ensure the delivery of the message, and Coz being there, I told the girl to mention 'Parrots' and to ask for two dollars.

I'd met him in prison while he was on remand for bird smuggling. The stories he told me were at times hard to believe; about the status of people he bought from and sold to. But one feature of his tales never varied: Coz said he always dispatched birds to his overseas customers from Townsville in Queensland. It was what I counted on. Hoping to collect on a prison favour, I bought a ticket to Frankston.

Waiting to change trains at Flinders street station, the trip took a nosedive. Someone there recognised me and if not as an 'enemy' then certainly not as a friend! It was tense all the while. Luckily I wasn't on the platform when it occurred, but in the cafeteria eating a sandwich. A man stared at me before hurrying out, to prop nearby in the crowded concourse—watching!

The sandwich finished, I 'strolled' out, anxious over what

to expect. A glance down at my watch, pretending surprise, then double-checking the station-clock, I rushed towards the exit-barriers, the milling crowd protecting me. Out through the turnstiles—wasting my ticket—I sped down the steps and turned abrupt left. The startled look I saw on the watcher's face was enough to confirm my suspicions.

Into a tiny shop not ten paces from the corner I rushed, dropping my bag to rummage through it, watching the window. And when he passed I stood up, to stride back the way I had just run, pulling a beret on before removing my glasses. I bought another ticket to Frankston.

+ + +

When I arrived no one waited to greet me. The few cars in the car-park dwindled quickly, leaving with their intended passengers while I, striving to appear nonchalant, walked away from the station stiff-legged, angry, not knowing which direction led to Coz's place; wondering if it was safe to continue.

A powerful motorbike cruised past me: it's helmeted rider, with army coat flapping, kicked down a gear, then turned and came back behind me. I dropped the bag to the footpath, squatting in haste, I plunged my hand deep inside to grip the reassuring Bulldog! Every muscle tensed as the bike stopped beside me.

The rider pushed up the helmet's visor to say, "How are ya, Joe? Long time no see." I glimpsed Coz's broken-tooth smile and all through me a warm feeling of relief coursed.

I shook hands, enjoying his easy speech. "In a bit of

bother then, mate?" He opined as he unclipped a helmet behind him. "I thought it might 'a been you left the message." He handed the helmet to me. "Hop on," he said.

The hard-hat in hand, I asked, "Are you sure? If my being here is a problem mate –"

"Struth no!" he interjected. He grabbed my bag, positioning it on the tank between his thighs, brooking no argument. "A bloody pleasure, mate." I climbed on behind, wrestling the helmet on.

✛ ✛ ✛

After ten minutes of Kamikaze riding and then bouncing down a gravel road, we finally swung into the driveway of an old farmhouse set well back. I sprang off, relieved, and grabbed my bag. Coz pushed the bike into a tin shed.

Leading me to the back door, Coz explained, "There's only me mum and sister live here with me, Joe, so make yourself at home."

Nodding to him, I replied, "Thanks mate." What else could I say in the face of such trust?

"Jane's a lot older than me," he remarked as we entered the house. "Near your age, and she's great. Only don't tell me mum anything—she's a bit of a worrier, mate."

His mother bustled about in the kitchen preparing the evening meal while his sister, sitting in the lounge-room, sketched a small lizard in a fish tank. Coz left me with Jane in silence until he returned with beers.

"I haven't done birds for over a year," he explained after sitting down. Then confided, "It's reptiles now, Joe.

That's how we sussed it was you," indicating Jane, letting me know that she was up to speed. "How can we help ya?"

Coz hasn't changed at all, I thought. He's still as straightforward and friendly as ever. The idea of their being imprisoned if caught-out helping me had probably not crossed his mind! A feeling of shame came to pass as I remembered that I had set out to manipulate him.

Dinner was a help-yourself affair and, with his mum popping in non-sequiturs every second sentence, my transport problem had not been stated. Interrupting her mum, Jane asked if I would like to see a herpetarium—I was being told in minute detail how kidney stones are removed—with Coz nodding for me to agree. I obediently said yes and away we sped, leaving their mum quite miffed!

For an hour we drove in Jane's car, with a park on the beach and not a snake pit seen, talking and laughing like old friends planning a holiday. They were taking me to Queensland, ha-ha.

That night I slept like a babe under the protective roof of their old home. I'm not surprised Christians were fed to lions in the Roman days!

WITHIN MINUTES OF OUR CROSSING THE MURRAY RIVER, THE HEADLIGHTS OF A HIGHWAY-PATROL CAR RACED UP BEHIND US

✛ ✛ ✛

Tuesday was comfortably filled with activity in preparation for our trip. Their telephone (an unlisted number) ran hot with them reorganising their days ahead. Food and such were packed to last us all the way. At dusk, his mum kissed me goodbye, whispering that she wished we had met in better circumstances. The old dear had known all along!

+ + +

WEDNESDAY 9TH JULY
ECHUCA, VIC

By the time we crossed the Victorian border into New South Wales, the next day had begun. Ensconced on the rear seat, I finally settled back, feeling secure at last. But not for long.

Within minutes of our crossing the Murray River, the headlights of a highway-patrol car raced up behind us, the policeman in it signalling Jane to pull over. I sat stunned, shocked... till the grey matter got firing.

It has to be a traffic violation, I reasoned; nothing else made sense. Never the less I shit myself—not literally, but I came close. And in nervous reaction I crept my hand into the bag beside me to clutch the Bulldog.

Jane slowed the car while I kept her calm (as well as myself) by reiterating what had been rehearsed before we set out, in case of just such an event. To have as a destination, we had memorised a few names and addresses in three major towns on our route, and we had planned for her to nag him about lost points if booked for an offence. If asked, she was to add that I was a friend of her brother's whom she was driving interstate as a favour.

In the rear-vision mirror, I watched Jane greet the pa-
trolman halfway back. By the blaze of his high beams, he
studied her driver's license... then walked towards our car,
swinging his torch, his revolver holstered high on his hip.
Like a rubber band stretched, I waited, balls up tight. No way
did I intend to use the Bulldog—it was a liability here, not
an asset! I jerked my hand out, and felt strangely calm after
having done that.

Signs of relief washed Coz's face. So he was aware of the
risks taken! I smiled at him just as the torch-beam lit me up.

"Would you mind, officer?" I complained, lifting my
hand to shield my face. "That light is very bright." My heart
thumped like a drum. The light swung to Coz... then back
to me! And the beam flicked off.

Jane conned him perfectly. She later explained to us
while cutting across to another highway, how he had lec-
tured her instead of giving her a ticket when she had admitted her misdeed. Apparently, when driving too fast over the
bridge at Echuca, a sharp dog-leg had forced her to cross
double-lines momentarily; a minor point, but the cause of
our being halted!

After that they believed me when I asserted: "It's little
mistakes like that, which usually bring people undone."

We breakfasted in the flatlands of New South Wales off
the roadway under a canopy of gum trees. Jane and Coz dos-
sed in the car while I, using the car-rug and my trusty bag
as a pillow, tiredly bedded down a hundred metres out from
them, to sleep Thursday's sunshine away.

✛ ✛ ✛

TELEX 10(Thurs) 7(July) 1980 Qld

MARYBOROUGH. Break-in of Hotel . . .
safe burnt open... $10,000 in cash . . .
MARYBOROUGH. Attempted break-in
of Golf-club... nothing stolen

THURSDAY 10TH JULY 1980
NEW SOUTH WALES

We passed through the rest of NSW, without further incident. A circuitous nine hundred kilometres were travelled in one swift night. We refuelled before dawn at Bogga-Billa, crossing the Queensland border at Goondiwindi. Jane followed a dirt road until it petered out near a billabong, where we made our camp: it was a peaceful spot with birds chirping their morning songs, and a crisp dryness in the air. So different from Victoria's wet.

Friday's morning-sun rose while we ate, enjoying its company around the cook fire. And after cleaning up, we swam and splashed the early morning away till finally we sprawled in exhausted sleep on the thick carpet of grass bordering the water.

+ + +

FRIDAY 11TH JULY 1980
QUEENSLAND

That evening, dinner was a three-course meal enjoyed with wine and song in a hotel at Miles: followed by a leisurely night drive through Taroom and on to Biloela for petrol. Then inland west under a myriad of stars to eventually stop before Saturday's sunrise, at a camping-ground, just north of Emerald.

Eggs and bacon, sausages and tomatoes—a truckies breakfast if ever I've had one! And there I slept until noon.

TELEX 11(Fri) 7(July) 1980 Qld.

SARINA. Break and enter of a Police
Station... safe opened with key ...
7 revolvers and 'cuffs stolen.

✚ ✚ ✚

SATURDAY 12TH JULY 1980
QUEENSLAND

My real purpose and destination—to link up with Fritz at Bowen—stayed unknown to Coz and Jane: and not because I distrusted them. Far from it! I kept it secret because they did not need to know. I felt confident and secure not telegraphing my moves. To them Mackay was the end of the line.

With a slight nudge from me we set off at mid-day... till in the afternoon, leaving Nebo behind, Mackay came into sight. On the city's outskirts at a truckies petrol stop, we drank coffee and talked in its eatery.

I sat at the table in a quandary, wondering if an offer of money would insult the two; or if payment was the answer, how to go about it to avoid tarnishing their act of kindness? Jane saved me from any blunder.

"We owe you an awful lot, Joe," she began in earnest. "And your paying for everything on the way up isn't what I'm referring to." My surprise only spurred her on. "Coz told mum and me how you stood up for him in the prison and how—"

"Come off it, Jane!" Cut in Coz, embarrassed by her unexpected frankness. "Why bring that up?"

Jane spoke softly to him, "It has to be said... so he knows why we helped." She turned to me. "None of us knew what to expect—but we've all heard ugly stories about prison. And him being so young at the time, it worried mum sick. Then he told us about you." Jane bobbed across the table and kissed me on the cheek.

Coz and I quickly turned the subject to the coast drive back. It's really odd how when we most want to hug some-one, we tend to veer aside from emotion. They were true-blue!

+ + +

Watching them drive south, a tear in my heart, I wished them well. For those few days in their company I had almost forgotten that I was one of the ten-most-wanted men in Australia. That moment cemented the resolution I had made descending the hills of Adelaide: to think and act as a free person (within reason) and not as a man pursued.

Sitting there in the evening sun, I watched an elderly couple pull into the bowsers from the south, their car packed full of boxes and suitcases on top. While the guy filled up the petrol tank and the old lady toddled off to the toilet area, I strolled over to ask him for a lift to Bowen if they were go-ing that way.

"My wife and I," he said, "are going to Townsville to vis-it our daughter." Then offered, "you're welcome to ride with us to Bowen, if you don't mind squeezing in the back."

I grabbed my bag and squeezed onto the box-laden rear seat, happy with the luck of an old couple for company and camouflage, and looking forward to seeing the ocean again.

After returning to the car, the old lady relaxed back in the front seat and smiled at me in greeting as though I had always sat there in the rear! A non-stop barrage of idle chat-ter and probing questions, coffee and sandwiches, held me spellbound all the way to Bowen where I left them, breathing a sigh of relief. They were a lovely couple, but a contradiction to my enforced life-style. And so trusting!

By eight o'clock, I had located Fritz at the beach: then back to a motel to book in for the night. A take-away consumed with a bottle of red on the beach was dinner, a hot shower, then in to bed and off to sleep with the tinkle of Fritz showering in the background.

✚ ✚ ✚

SUNDAY 13TH JULY
SOUTH QUEENSLAND

Leaving the motel at Bowen was as uneventful as our entering of it. We were on the highway, eating up the kilometres, before the towns-people had finished breakfast.

Fritz is a logical thinker and is also a compulsive man, so when he stated that his van had to be serviced the next day, I knew he meant it. I argued that we should wait till Cairns, but in his annoying way his persistence won. The town he selected was Ingham, 300 kilometres further north in sugarcane country.

At Ayr, Fritz washed dirty clothes in the laundromat while I took a nervous constitutional through the township. The laundromat stands opposite the police station and anything was preferable to bustling about in that rat-trap like Fritz, pushing his luck. It wasn't till after we left Ayr that I learnt Fritz had been completely unaware of the risk he took! But that was typical of Fritz.

After a few hours of scenic driving, we ate lunch while rubber-necking our way along the Townsville mall, observing the motley lot of Aboriginals who seemed to fill the complex. But the bad vibes in that city soon had us in the van and again moving north.

The mode of travel chosen by Fritz made him independent of motels and such, but the idea of leaving his camper in a service-station all day, loaded to the gunnels with his accumulated possessions was anathema to him. A rented caravan was a must, Fritz said. So that evening at about 5:30 pm we pulled into the Ingham caravan-park. This decision of his, its importance unrealised, would wait like the part of a time-piece until fifteen months later, when it would mesh together with others in a way no-one could possibly have foreseen!

The owner of this park was a retired Justice of the Peace who had an excellent memory and was an insomniac: three unusual characteristics in one man, of which two were to play a vital part that night. The third (his probity) came to bear much later—but first, the facts.

Fritz booked us in for two nights—Sunday and Monday—and while signing the book, he asked the owner for a baking-dish. It was agreed that one would be supplied.

Later that evening, when the dish arrived, the owner was aghast and then irate over the amount of boxes and bags and personal effects crammed inside his caravan! The purpose was painstakingly explained to him by Fritz and, if not pleased then at least satisfied, the owner left us. This chance stop cast the temporal set.

If not for the Bowen motel and the Ingham caravan-park, proof would never have surfaced to conclusively establish the vans route and timetable. And when required in a courtroom, we produced that Ace to prove where we were that Sunday night!

+ + +

TELEX 14(Mon) 7(July) 1980 Qld.

ROCKHAMPTON.
Break enter and steal...
Hotel safe burnt open . . .
$13,000 stolen . . .

MONDAY 14TH JULY
CENTRAL QUEENSLAND

Fritz rose before the sun did. He strapped his pushbike to the van before driving away to the town's centre.

I lay there in comfortable half-slumber until I heard Fritz bang his bike against the caravan. I filled the jug to make a brew as he came in with the milk. And the manager called out a friendly, "G'day folks!"

During breakfast we itemised our needs for the day. I wanted to buy clothes and a shoulder bag, and Fritz needed to re-victual his van. We set out strolling the town, buying what was required as we saw it, and we counter-lunched at the main hotel. In the afternoon, Fritz drove his 'home' back to the caravan-park while I walked to savour the day.

Together we perused the van's 10,000 kilometres service-report. The time-clock's imprint showed 8:05 am Monday 14th July 1980. The signature for its receipt, and the signature in the caravan-park's ledger, matched the specimen in Fritz's bank account. Neither of us knew then how vital the *false* vehicle-registration and *false* bank account were to be (Fritz soon-after adopted a new alias), but when exhumed they were of inestimable value!

That evening, Fritz and I dined out in the Roma café: fish, red wine, and songs; then back to the caravan-park. We re-loaded the Volkswagen before hitting the sack.

+ + +

TUESDAY 15TH JULY
CENTRAL QUEENSLAND

The morning drive up through the hills north of Ingham is one I will always remember. Being a Victorian, I found the contrast of dense mangrove-swamp below with rain forest above a stirring sight—we were just as much tourists as the others parked on top of that range. The locals speeding by were easily identified by their haste and yahoo comments.

The scenery simply got better and greener the further we progressed along the Bruce highway. In fits and starts, we proceeded to Innisfail where we halted for lunch at the Can-ecutters hotel alongside the Johnstone River. This town—or at least the region—we both agreed was an ideal place to settle. But first we had to go to Cairns to pick up our mail and for Fritz to re-register his camper van in Queensland. Regional I.D. is best to avoid being conspicuous.

As expected, Cairns is a tinsel city over-run by tour-ists, police, the drug-scene, and transients. After doing what we had to, we left as rapidly as decorum permitted, heading into the foothills of the Atherton tablelands where later, en-sconced in a picnic area at Kuranda, adjacent to a memorial steam engine, we cooked an al-fresco tea beneath the stars.

+ + +

WEDNESDAY 16TH JULY
NORTH QUEENSLAND

All day we drove around like tourists (which we were, really) getting a feel for the area as well as looking for a place to rent. The people were friendly and the weather was superb. We had dinner on the sand at Mission beach.

My sleep that night was the worst during the entire trip up from Melbourne. Don't ever let anyone convince you that a V.W. combi-van is built to comfortably sleep two. And if they try, I'll lay you fives' that they're attempting to sell it to someone!

✦ ✦ ✦

THURSDAY 17TH JULY
NORTH QUEENSLAND

With the day almost over and no expectation of any success on our second day's search for accommodation, we were told about a house for rent. The offer came out of the blue at a beach kiosk when we mentioned our desire of finding a place.

The house was small, on stilts, with no fence, and a two-minute walks from the beach. We were peering in the windows when the owner arrived in response to my phone-call, and handed me the keys to take a look inside. He was a cripple, so he stayed in his car but his Philipino wife came with us to extol the virtues of the house and the small community.

Chance chose who paid the rent and, consequently, became responsible in law for its contents at a later date. I handed her enough money for four weeks rent and her husband scribbled out a receipt. The name I used was Robert Abbot.

At last I had sanctuary, a place to think and feel safe. The house was mid-way between Innisfail and Tully, with a population of about 200—and no cop-shop. With the fridge stocked-up and the door-locks replaced, I relaxed, settling in to enjoy life touring the area with Fritz, visiting all the beaches, even travelling as far north as Cape Tribulation to hob-nob with the hippies never for a moment visualising the travails yet to unfold!

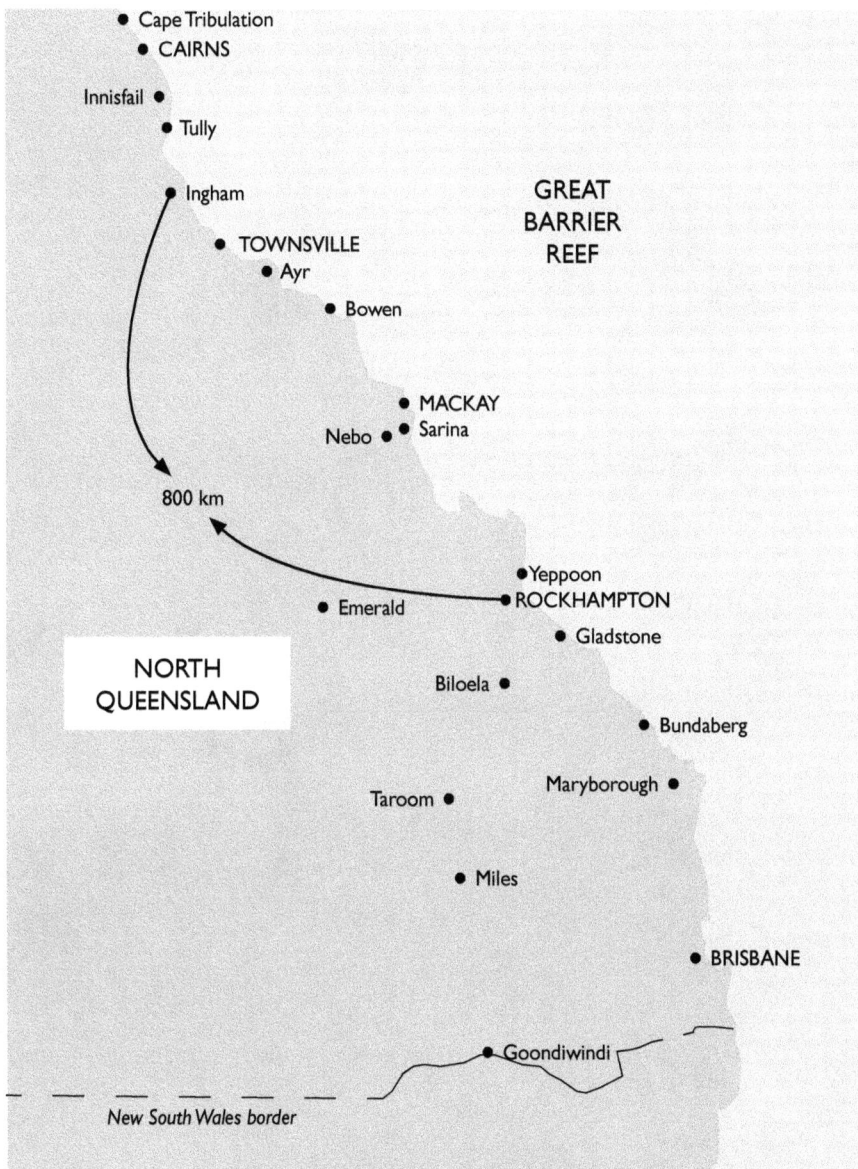

Cape Tribulation
CAIRNS
Innisfail
Tully
Ingham

GREAT
BARRIER
REEF

TOWNSVILLE
Ayr
Bowen

MACKAY
Nebo Sarina

800 km

Yeppoon
ROCKHAMPTON
Emerald
Gladstone

NORTH
QUEENSLAND

Biloela

Bundaberg

Maryborough

Taroom

Miles

BRISBANE

Goondiwindi

New South Wales border

▲ Map of travels through North Queensland

RE-CAPTURE

TRUTH IS WRITTEN IN SHIFTING SAND

TUESDAY 25TH NOVEMBER 1980
KURRIMINE BEACH NORTH QUEENSLAND

My capture was anti-climatic. Three cars carrying seven police drove onto the front lawn while I, oblivious to their
arrival, sanded rust spots off a utility I'd purchased in Cairns.
The lead car held three plainclothes; the two tailing cars each
carried two uniforms.

I stood surrounded by police. Not because I dropped my
guard, not because of information nor sedulous investigation, but by an unlikely set of circumstances. They came to
me investigating a user/seller of drugs whose former known
address was where I resided. Hoping to glean information
about a forwarding address, a search warrant had been issued
two days prior for the house, in case the occupant (me) failed

to cooperate. How can you win?

I have never smoked and I rarely drink—yet here I appeared in the minds of those around me a suspect of being, or at least associated with, a drug-user. It was beyond me!

Suppressing my shock and disbelief, I accompanied the three detectives through the rear doorway of the house, to stand in the kitchen. The uniforms stayed outside.

The senior Detective asked, "What is your name, please?" While the other two, one a female, began rummaging about in the food cupboard.

"Robert Abbott," I answered. "I'm a Victorian, holidaying up here until Christmas.

"Then this is not your house?"

"No, it isn't. I'm only renting it."

"Well then, Mister Abbott, you're responsible for its contents." Then asked, "Are those motor vehicles yours?" waving his hand to indicate the utility, and a Buick parked behind the house along with a caravan and a motorbike.

"No, they're not," I half lied. "The ute belongs to a mate, Ken Goldsworthy (the false name I used when registering the utility). He's working in Cairns until the end of the month." Adding, "The Buick belongs to my girlfriend," doing my best to appear helpful. I had met Colleen at Yeppoon three months earlier and had invited her to stay with me at Kurrimine: a fortuitous invitation that later helped me in court.

"And where is she, Mister Abbott?" he probed, searching underneath the sink. The female detective now stood in the doorway, blocking egress to the outside.

I promptly offered, "She's at the beach," knowing full well that Colleen had gone to wash clothes at the near-by caravan park. The third detective inquired, "Which bedroom is yours?" He had finally finished ratting through the food-cupboard and now stood undecided in front of the two bedroom doors; mine open and Fritz's closed.

I replied, "The one you're looking in now." The whole event had disconcerted me—all I could do was delay them until I caught up mentally. He entered the bedroom, leaving me with the other two in silence.

Outside the bluebottles were enthusiastically searching the cars. A lot of banging noise filtered through before one of them came inside and asked me for the key to unlock the caravan.

I told him, "It's not my van, officer. I don't have a key to it," trying not to look at the key ring hanging off a nail above the stove. The caravan and all of the contents of it belonged to Fritz, and he was somewhere in New South Wales.

"Break it open," ordered the senior Jack to the uniform. Then to me: "Do you have identification?"

I responded, "Certainly!" not the least bit confident inside. Wallet in hand, I removed my false licence. "Is this sufficient? If not I have more in the bedroom." I handed it over.

He studied it and said, "It will do for now."

"Sarge!" came the demanding call from within my bedroom. "Will you come in here?" The sinking of my stomach portended what was coming. To cover her nervousness, the female, now alone with me, asked an idle question or two—but all I could wonder about was what are those two going to find?

Appearing in the bedroom's doorway, the Sergeant asked, "Is this weapon yours, Mister Abbott?" There was a tremor in his voice. The other detective stood close behind him.

"Shit, no!" I exclaimed. Exactly what I wished not

I KNEW I SHOULD NEVER HAVE KEPT THAT FUCKING GUN!

to see—the Bulldog! He held it upside down by the trigger-guard, confronting me with it. "It's not mine, Sergeant!" my pent-up frustration pouring out in protest. "I've never seen it before!" Like, what else could I say? I knew I should never have kept that fucking gun!

They disappeared out of my sight, back into the bedroom. The female entered the kitchen further, unblocking the door—and I bolted!

"He's running away!" she bellowed out. Banal I'll agree, but that is what she cried as I dashed for freedom through the cordon of blue. By racing away, I gave myself a slim chance of eluding them, where-as by staying at the house, I had no chance what-so-ever.

Pursuit was instantaneous. Within minutes I thought I had the edge on them—and the fitness—so I raced on. I sped through back yards; along two streets; on past the last house; across a road and down into a wide clay-pan. Heart and lungs in pain, I clambered up its other side and sprawled to a suddenly painful halt. I lay spread-eagled in small bushes, ankle twisted in my own frantic haste.

Ankle on fire, I scrambled to my feet. But when up right I heard a menacing voice, shockingly close to me shout, "Halt! Halt or I'll fire!"

He stood less than ten metres to my left, feet spread and revolver aimed, prepared to shoot me. I stared down the gun-barrel and having been shot three times previously, I did not relish the painful experience a fourth time. Sweet success soured to failure.

I had forgotten to calculate that while a few chased me on foot, the remainder would not sit and twiddle their thumbs! A police car had been used to maximum advantage.

My brain throbbing, I limped back to the car on lead-filled legs where the waiting driver handcuffed my wrists behind my back, before shoving me unceremoniously into the rear. With the gun rammed into my ribs I exchanged insults with the two all the way back to the house.

"Sit down and don't move!" yelled the trembling Sergeant as soon as I walked in. "You're under arrest!"

"What am I charged with?" I demanded. "I'm entitled to know what the charge is!"

"You attempted to escape," he snapped. "And you'll be charged with that for a start." He shook with anger.

"But officer, I wasn't under arrest at the time!" I protested. "No-one told me I couldn't leave the house."

He stared at me, unsure of my attitude. "So you think you know the law, do you."

The other detective barked at me: "Sit down, smart arse! You'll be charged with the revolver—that's enough to lock you up." He confirmed what I suspected; they still had no idea of my true identity. I sat down.

The adrenalin rush from the chase had kept me from plummeting into an emotional pit of despair. It is either a feeling of panic or one of desolation when arrested. My state of mind was somewhere in between.

While the female watched me lizard-eyed, the two detectives and a uniformed cop really tossed my bedroom over. Before long, the senior Jack opened Fritz's door to enter, then asked me, "Whose bedroom is this?"

"The owner of the utility I told you about," ad-libbing to my earlier lie. "I think you should wait till you ask him."

"It will be searched now," he stated, taking me seriously. "The warrant is for drugs and we will search the entire house."

As they filed into the bedroom, I angrily remarked, "Well I'm not responsible for that room's contents!" I had no idea what might be in there, so I tried to cover myself just to be safe.

From where I sat at the kitchen table, I watched one of them rifle through a plethora of documents in a suitcase: the other two emptied the contents of bags and drawers onto the floor until one looked up, and pushed the door to block my view. Regardless of what else might be found, I would be taken away and charged. But some good would arise out of it: when I failed to make my nightly phone-call to Melbourne, Fritz would be alerted that something was amiss and act accordingly.

The object now was to conceal my true identity from them until they locked me up for the night. But what I failed to for-see was what they were already beginning to suspect; my lack of mental dislocation indicated some prior experience with bullying police!

They trooped out of the bedroom to talk with the others who came in, then stared at me, their looks ominous. "There's a lot of property in this house," began the Sergeant. "And I suspect that a lot of it is stolen; the documentation in that last room for example." He went on to say, "Also an amount of marijuana has been located in one of the cars, and a pistol."

The pistol and marijuana I knew about—they belonged to Colleen.

The image of Fritz puffing on a joint was ludicrous!

I asked, "Which car were they found in?" to be interrupted by a flurry of activity at the back door... and in strode Colleen!

"Hello," she greeted everyone as she blithely came to me at the kitchen-table and sat down, completely ignoring the roomful of menace! Her spunk delighted me; though I wished she had stayed away. Now she would be subjected to questioning too. The oddity was that Coll had no knowledge of me being a prison escapee. Certainly she had questioned that not all was on the up-and-up, but accepted my explanation that my unsocial habits were due to a psychological problem I suffered from.

The Sergeant demanded, "Who are you?" of Colleen, but she ignored him, giving me her full attention, while we conversed in undertones.

"Do you live here?" he persisted, moving in close to her. The Sergeant's proximity had spoiled my attempt to convince Coll to claim $1000 in our bedroom as her own; and to retain a solicitor for me. She had no money to speak of.

"What's happening here has nothing to do with Colleen," I calmly pointed out. "Please don't hassle her."

This time the Sergeant spoke more civilly: "Is the white sedan yours, Colleen?"

"Yes it is, officer," she flatly replied, her upper-class accent in every word. "Why do you ask?"

"Under the Health Act your Buick has been searched. Do you have proof of ownership?"

She grudged him an answer. "I do. Bob has it."

"YOU FILTHY PIG!" I VEHEMENTLY STATED. "HASSLE HER AND YOU'LL GET NOTHING BUT PROBLEMS OUT OF ME!"

I got Colleen to remove my wallet and hand it to him. As she did, the others watched like predatory birds in on a kill.

I explained, "The receipt for her car is in the back section."

He studied the slip and then addressed Colleen. "Can you prove to me that you are this person?" She gave him a disdainful look and no reply.

"You'll answer my questions at the police station when —" began his threat. But before his words had finished, I forcefully kicked the table, scattering every article on it to the floor!

"You filthy pig!" I vehemently stated. "Hassle her and you'll get nothing but problems out of me!" A few more words were spat out before I settled down on a chair as though nothing had occurred.

My belligerent display while handcuffed really surprised them. And, of course, I had blown it for myself. So much for wise intent!

"Answer his questions," I advised Colleen. "You can't harm me with the truth."

Then after a brief conversation, part of which involved the money in my wallet being handed to Colleen, she went with the Sergeant into our bedroom to indicate her belongings.

Only a few minutes passed before they returned. The Sergeant had a deal to offer. "Colleen won't be taken away from here, nor charged, if you cooperate. Do you agree to that?"

Strangely enough, I sensed that he really meant it. Appeasingly I replied, "Yes, of course I will," though not for a moment agreeing to the kind of cooperation he wanted in return for Colleen's freedom: admissions to what-ever criminal charges emerged. Not likely!

The woman detective left the house and quickly reversed a car up to the front door. They bundled me out, into the rear seat with a detective each side and drove rapidly away. A queasy coldness filled me, like my blood being drained out. Shock, I supposed it to be.

+ + +

At the highway, 12 kilometres from the house, the car swung north. They were not taking me to the nearest police station at Silkwood, as I had believed and hoped they would—Fritz and I had set-up the cell block so that we could get out. Blocking out the distracting fears, I strove to centre my mind, donning mental armour that had protected me as a street-wise teenager and later from the mind-games perpetrated on a daily basis in prison.

My re-imprisonment now was a fait accompli and my return to Yatala prison would only be a matter of time, subject to my conduct and what charges were preferred. I therefore decided during the fifteen-minute drive to Innisfail to try and lull them into allowing me a solicitor.

+ + +

We can all be wise in retrospect, from the comfort of an armchair with time to spare and a drink in our hand; but to be wise at the time, under the pressure of arrest, borders on genius. In my lifetime I have met only a few who have that ability, so I'm not Robinson Crusoe when I admit to the human flaw of permitting hope and fair play to creep in and muddle-up my decision making. Expecting to be afforded the protection of the law in custody, I intended to exercise my legal rights. A naïve expectation.

✛ ✛ ✛

"I must have your real name!" the Sergeant demanded of me for the third time. I sat behind a desk in a large room at the front of the police station. "Do you understand me?" He shook a hand-full of papers in my face, unsuccessful in trying to frighten me.

My concern was more for my hands than answering his questions. They felt numb behind my back—the 'cuffs had cut off their circulation during the car trip in, and both shoulders hurt. The Sergeant poked my chest. "We'll find out you know," he asserted, "when we take your fingerprints." He stalked away, to sit at a desk and pick up a phone.

That caught my attention. I asked, "Are you suggesting that I have a criminal record?" Then snapped at him, "You are aren't you!"

"I'm not suggesting anything of the sort," he retorted. "But I must have your true identity." All three watched me expectantly.

"You do have it, officer," I blandly put to him. "And

when I see a solicitor, I'll be able to prove it to you."

While he digested that, I asked THE question. every nuance under control: "Do I telephone a solicitor, or do you do it for me?"

He answered with finality. "I'll decide that after we take your fingerprints," and again sat at his desk.

In an angry reply, I cried, "You'll have to break my fingers to get them! I'm not a bloody criminal!" My volte-face startled him to his feet. "I demand my right to legal advice and it's your duty to grant it!" They all stared in surprise, surveying me in silence.

I curbed my emotions enough to ask, "Do I get a solicitor, Sergeant, or not?" I had to safeguard myself from abuse when special-squad pigs took my case off the locals once my status became known.

"Yes, all right," he begrudgingly said. "I'll ring the Court's duty-solicitor for you."

My suspicions allayed, they escorted me to the lock-up and removed the 'cuffs. Into a bag went my ring, watch and belt, then down to an empty cell I went like a man for the gallows who has been reprieved for a day.

The cell stunk. An overpowering smell wafted off the pedestal and grotty blankets. I kicked it all into the toilet's corner and retreated to another to hunch down, optimistic, trying to generate constructive thought.

They had missed my money-belt and I was grateful, because I now had cash up-front. But best of all, being granted a solicitor, I no longer had the gnawing fear of my identity being uncovered before I gained legal protection. I resigned myself to wait… that small spark of hope burning bright… yeah, I believed him.

✚ ✚ ✚

Fifteen or maybe twenty hour-long minutes crept by till I again heard keys in the cell block. At last!

Before the cell-door opened I was up and ready to go. Three uniforms filled the doorway and one, the key holder, said, "The Sergeant wants to talk with you." He beckoned me out and I promptly obliged.

No sooner had I cleared the doorframe than I was grabbed by the uniforms, one on each arm and speared into another two waiting in the passageway. What happened frightened me and though I did not retaliate physically, I did protest verbally. And then a fat pig pounced from behind and reefed my head back in a stranglehold, my air supply choked off.

The shock! It gave me extra strength as we wrestled our way towards the detectives.

With the others latched onto my arms and legs, subduing me, this fat scumbag worked his forearm in under my chin and squeezed! Pure panic. Of course I fought then. I thought he was trying to kill me—the moron was crushing my larynx!

I struggled in earnest, desperate to force his forearm to the side of my throat. His elbow in front (the correct position for a sleeper hold), I plunged into unconsciousness, my skull pounding red waves of pain.

I PLUNGED INTO UNCON-SCIOUSNESS, MY SKULL POUNDING RED WAVES OF PAIN

I came to… and the pressure reapplied! Before losing consciousness again I felt them remove my shoes and shorts, searching for identification marks and mouthing snide remarks.

I came to… as one of them was chortling over the discovery of my money-belt. I moved to untwist my body—and that fat slob again choked the life out of me!

I came to… lying on my stomach with them all over me like cockroaches, while a detective manipulated my left hand, taking fingerprint impressions. I lay defeated, scared of being killed by incompetence, filling my lungs with what scant air I could suck into my tortured body.

Turning me over, they continued on with my humiliation, at least six of them, in agreement with what went on. They could have sodomised me that day. There was nothing I could have done to prevent it! From that experience I learnt exactly what a woman goes through before she is gang-raped and because of that, if ever I encounter that fat swine alone, I will cripple him irrespective of his age and the legal consequences!

When it finally ended, they dragged me to an even filthier cell and, tossing my clothes on the floor, locked me in to recover from the assault. My torn muscles pained when I moved, but that was nothing compared to how my throat hurt! Denied water to ease the blockage, I coughed spasmodically and spat out blood well into the night, long after the sounds of the town had faded into silence.

For hours I crouched in the lighted cell castigating myself, knowing that worse was yet to come. And if I slept at all that night, it was in fits and starts without a blanket—and cold—a softening up technique of which I had previous experience. Distance had deluded me into expecting police conduct to improve as one travelled north.

✦ ✦ ✦

The morning started early with the handing out of breakfast to the other prisoners, though not to me. I banged on the door demanding a drink of water and got what I expected—abuse. As the sounds of that faded away I prowled the cell, thirsty. I even looked into the toilet; but only a loony contemplating suicide would have drunk from it.

An exercise workout eased all the muscle stiffness and, except for my sore throat, I felt well enough to shrug off the worry of them returning for a second bout.

Keys rattling outside the door warned me that someone was near. The small food-trap dropped and the Sergeant put his face to the hole. "We know who you are, Joe. It's been confirmed," he said.

Exactly what I expected to hear after the print-taking farce, but still, I experienced a loss when he put it into words. "A Telex from South Australia came in confirming it this morning."

I asked, "What happens now?" The somberness of the moment stole my thoughts.

"You'll be going into court at ten o'clock," he explained, "to be remanded to Townsville prison. Do you understand the procedure?"

"Yes. What am I charged with?"

"The guns and the marijuana, Joe; that's all. Unless you give us a cause, you'll be gone from here this afternoon." He then asked, "Are you going to make trouble for us in the court today?"

"No." I gave the concession: "I'll go along with that," thinking, the quicker to Townsville prison the safer for me! "What's happened to Colleen?" Spontaneously I voiced concern for her welfare.

"Orders were given by me for Colleen to be left alone. If she comes in and the hearing ends quickly," he promised, "I'll let her visit you for a few minutes, okay?" That final offer is what got me on side.

"Yeah,' I agreed, falling in line with his wont instead of my own. "But keep that fat pig away from me!"

"Okay, Joe," he said. "We have a deal then. See you at ten o'clock." The trap in the door slammed shut.

My thoughts were turbid, but one thing I sensed clearly was that the conversation left me troubled; a doubt I unwisely over-ruled. I paced the cell, releasing some of my pent-up uncertainty.

✛ ✛ ✛

When next they entered the block, I knew it was near ten o'clock. My door opened last and two unknown detectives stepped in brandishing handcuffs. Outside in the passageway, other prisoners were being readied for court. They led me out, expecting me to go straight to the gate and be first across to the courthouse as directed. Instead, I made a beeline to the sink!

I must have guzzled a litre of water while sluicing my face and neck under the tap. Some hurry-up commands were made but I ignored the lot, trying to gauge their attitude. They seemed to be reasonable men, doing their job.

With two prisoners in the lead, I followed them into the small dock of the Magistrates court. A score of people filled the courtroom—and Colleen was not in sight.

My feeling of isolation grew. Unfortunately for me, I tend to adopt a siege mentality when under threat; which is why I didn't (poor cousin to an excuse) bellow out like a bull in pain that day!

The charges were read: "Did have in his possession a quantity of cannabis, a drug of dependence. And under the Firearms Act did unlawfully possess two handguns: a point-25 pistol and a point-38 revolver? The calibre quoted for the bulldog-snub was an understandable error, I thought. A five-shot 45 is similar in size to a six-shot 38. No doubt their mistake would be rectified at the next hearing. The rest of the remand application also captured my attention:

"The prisoner is an escapee from Yatala prison in South Australia, Your Worship. If bail is sought it will be opposed on that basis."

The Magistrate didn't even bother to look at me or offer me right of reply. "Bail is refused. Remanded to appear here on the twenty-eighth of November. Remove the prisoner."

The over-riding concern to see Colleen barely quelled my tongue's angry retort. The purpose of an obligatory appearance before a court within twenty-four hours of one's arrest is to ensure that a prisoner's rights are upheld. My taciturnity and his bias conspired to defeat the law—and I wasn't even asked if I was really me!

Back in the watch-house the Sergeant's nice-guy role was dropped. "You will be held here until we've completed our enquiries," he gloated. "Some boys from Brisbane want to interview you."

I grokked it in one—Special Squad pigs were coming! All the promises had been lies, given to keep me quiet in their court. They now had me legally for three days! I spat on his retreating back as the door slammed shut; its knell of doom ringing out long after the sound had fled the cell.

✛ ✛ ✛

Two hours later, the cell door was unlocked and slammed open. In barged a large pox-faced detective, tailed by a sour-faced companion who stated aggressively, "We're from the Crime Investigation Branch, Brisbane. My name's Railer and this is detective Pinko. We've been in contact with South Australia, so we know all about you and what your go is." Railer pushed his face forward, his beady eyes trying to stare me down. "But it won't work here! Either you give it to us straight—or it's a verbal! Got that?" His tone of voice spoke volumes.

My first words were, "What do you mean?" I did my best not to show fear. These two were capable of anything.

"First off, we want the Krauts whereabouts! And who it is he's travelling with!" Both detectives crowded in on me.

"I have no idea."

"Was the camper-van the only vehicle he had?" probed Railer, easing off on the menace.

"Yes," I quickly confirmed, knowing that he had a second van in New South Wales and by now should be in it.

"Did he have a trailer?" The very nature of the question

confirmed that they knew Fritz left towing one.

"Yes, he used it to carry petrol and prospecting gear as far as I know." (I had heard him telling a neighbour that before he left).

"Well do you know where he is?"

I answered truthfully, "I haven't seen him for more than two weeks. He could be anywhere." And now that my nightly phone-in was curbed, that was also true.

"Are you the owner of the utility?" Railer asked, changing the subject.

"No, I'm not. I use my girlfriend's car whenever I –"

"That's bullshit!" yelled Railer, full of venom. "It's already been checked out by the boys here—you bought that utility in Cairns. The sales rep picked your photo."

I knew that to be a lie: the rep told me he was leaving that week. The papers in the house told them the rest. I was now supposed to break down and admit to all. Not likely!

"I don't care what they say!" I loudly protested. "That utility is not mine!" Until they could prove that I bought it, a third person existed. And unless they questioned Colleen, it would take them a week to find out.

I exercised my legal right, not believing that it would be granted. "I want a solicitor in to advise me, please."

"Why? Do you have something to fear?" were Pinko's first words. I stared at him, wondering if that was a sarcastic joke. "Well, have you," he said. The glare in his eyes belied the offhandedness of his spoken words.

"No, I haven't. But I know this conversation is pointless without a solicitor to advise me. You have already said I'll be verballed if—"

"You won't be," Pinko quietly interposed. "Not if you

cooperate." He pulled out his notebook, and then made a big production of getting his pen ready. Either they suspected me of a serious crime, or information was sought.

I pointed out to them; "You're from a major-crime squad. I've done nothing on that scale to warrant interrogation by you. And I have no information about any."

Railer trounced me verbally. "You're an escapee, a known tankman, and you're in our fucking state!"

"But what's that got to do with –"

"Listen to me!" he raved on, overriding me. "Someone's been ripping open safes along the coast—and three police stations have gone off! You and that Kraut did them, or by Christ you know who did! Blank driver-licences located at the house and a federal-police gazette with your photo in it proves that you know something."

"Well, I didn't do them," I adamantly stated. (The documents were bought off a contact in Townsville who told me they came from a local detective on the take). I said, "I've lived in Kurrimine since July," and quick to clarify myself, added, "There's no way I've had anything to do with safes up here! Not all escapees are desperados." My comment got no reply.

Railer, reading from a slip of notepaper held by Pinko said, "You escaped from Yatala prison in June. What date did you rent the house?" The cell's unwashed walls glared, robbing me of inspiration.

"THERE'S NO WAY I'VE HAD ANYTHING TO DO WITH SAFES UP HERE! NOT ALL ESCAPEES ARE DESPERADOS."

"Mid July. I'm uncertain of the date."

"How did you travel through the states?"

"By combi-van." I had no intention of involving Coz and Jane. I knew Fritz would agree with me on that.

"So," snapped Pinko, "the Kraut did bring you up here!"

And Railer added, "We had information that he broke you out and that now confirms it."

Their knowing nods to each other angered me. "He had nothing to do with the break-in of Yatala!" These bastards are so quick to twist words to suit facts. "I met him much later; then travelled up here together."

Pinko asked, after perusing his bit of paper, "When were you in New South Wales?"

"The ninth or the tenth, I'm uncertain."

"Can you prove that you were there then?"

Unthinkingly, I replied, "Not really." Then realising my mistake, I quickly added, "But if I have to I'm sure I could find a witness or two!"

Railer stated, "And you entered Queensland at the Gold Coast?"

"No." I answered truthfully. "Inland at Goondiwindi."

Railer queried, "And then you went to Brisbane?"

"I never touched the coast until Mackay."

"What's that?" responded Pinko, surprised. My prompt and truthful reply surprised them at the time. (Later, I found out why!).

Pinko read aloud from his scrap of paper. "On Saturday the twelfth of July, a safe was blown open in Brisbane." He stared at me. "Where were you on that date?"

"At Bowen," I told them. "We stayed in a motel there

that night."

"Did you stay at any other motels coming up?" That question led my thoughts into a mental cul-de-sac. It locked me into motels!

"No," was my firm response.

"Anything else that you can think of to support your alibi?" urged Pinko. "Receipts, any place that required a signature, or people…"

"We slept out. There were no other places." Coz and Jane were still on my mind.

"You have partly confirmed our information that you couldn't have crossed the border to Victoria," Railer disclosed. "And that you came here direct from Adelaide."

"Yes, that's correct," I said, adopting the lie. The informants would be the Victorian police, not prepared to accept that I got past them and in to Melbourne!

"Can you think of anything at all Joe, which would confirm your own movements up through Queensland," urged Pinko. "We want this safe job in Brisbane cleared away as surely as you do." (The allegation of a crime in Brisbane was a red-herring - spurious. A common interrogation trick used to extract information for salting the verbal still to come.)

I did think about it too! Pinko had slipped the question in so casually that I never gave it the suspicion it deserved. My subconscious served me well. By not remembering the two days Fritz and I stayed at the Ingham caravan-park, I unwittingly preserved our best defence.

My answer came, after heavy thought, in the form of an apology: that an escapee, by nature, strives to leave no trail, no residue of self. I therefore had little to offer in support of my movements.

We boxed that around for a while before Railer, apt-
ly fitted to play the bad-guy role, put his presumptuous
attitude of guilty till proved innocent into words of accusation. "We know you robbed places to get money—you
were on the run—but what you did south doesn't interest
us. What you've done up here does!" He spat out more. "You
cut a safe at Rockhampton," (the first I knew of it). "And
probably the ones at Bundaberg and Maryborough too. But
the seven revolvers stolen from Sarina police station are what
we want back! Right? Give us them, or who's got them, and
you'll only get what you're right for—or you'll wear the
fucking lot!" He licked spittle from his lips. And if it was act-
ing, he fooled me.

"I've done nothing of the kind!" I vehemently protested.
"It wasn't us!" A futile request, but I had to ask it: "I want to
speak with a solicitor before I'm questioned any further."

"Fuck the solicitor!" raged Railer. "If you don't come
our way, I'll pull your sheila in and charge her with aiding
and abetting an escapee! How would you like that?"

Colleen's only crime was her innocence; I couldn't let
her be drawn into this madness. Their questions had been
chaff in the wind to winnow out of me a few seeds of fact
to salt a verbal and, as earlier stated, I withdraw when bad-
gered.

My knees shook slightly as I prepared myself, intent to
dispel any ideas they might harbour that I cared for Colleen.
"You gutless pig!" I laughed in his weasel face. "As if I give a
damn what you do to her! She's just a fuck." He shot back a
startled metre, a look of fear in his eyes.

Pinko quickly stepped into the gap, crashed his elbow
into my chest, pounding me backwards. "Right, that's done

it!" he yelled. I went straight to the floor, rolling away from Pinko's boot as it connected, lessening the force of his kick.

Railer stepped in, kicking me in the side and back as he shouted, "You're going to wear the lot for that, you bastard!"

They quickly tired of it. "Come away, Ugg!" panted Railer. "We've got enough to go on with; don't fuck about here with this mug." They sauntered away.

After the door slammed, I picked myself up off the floor and did a few limbering-up exercises to ease the pain and relieve the tension. My thoughts were clear as I reviewed my actions.

By provoking them, I had done myself a big favour. At least this way the damage was minimal and gave them little to go on... or so I thought. I was the meat in the sandwich, doing my best to kick the top slice off. I slumped in the corner, fully aware of what was in store for me. They are all the same. Violence was not the problem. What I feared mostly was what I lacked control over: words alleged to be mine! It is not what you say on the day, but what they say you said, that counts on the day in court.

✚ ✚ ✚

Jangling keys warned me. They were in the cell block! Turning to face the door, I waited... Alone... Scared... Awaiting the inevitable.

EPILOGUE

WHEN MEN ARE MOST SURE AND ARROGANT
THEY ARE COMMONLY MOST MISTAKEN

After more than eleven months on remand in Boggo Road prison, housed in a steel cage four steps by four steps with a small cell attached, I finally went to trial, charged with 23 offences. Townsville, Maryborough, Sarina, Bowen and Atherton, were some of the towns in which I was accused of committing offences.

To keep it brief and to the point, during the 54-day trial I endured, John J., my very able defence barrister, methodically tore into the Crown case. And in the latter half of the trial, when a witness with documented proof emerged and testified that Fritz and I were in the caravan park at Ingham on the evening of the 13th (the baking-dish witness with his ledger), and of the commencement time of the combi-van's service on the morning of the 14th, (stamped at 8:05 am), the case started to fall apart. To travel 800 kilometres from Ingham to Townsville, break into a hotel, cut a safe

▲ Boggo Road jail

▼ Inside of Boggo Road jail

open and then travel back to Ingham, all in twelve hours, was too much for the jury to accept. And as Fritz's trial barrister said to the Jury, "When the clock struck thirteen all that had preceded it was suss!" After that stage of the trial and the evidence that followed, the jury rejected all the charges relying on a confession. And how do I know that? The jury acquitted me of eighteen counts!

The 5-shot 45 Bulldog had metamorphosed into a 6-shot 38 Special from Sarina, but fortunately the Jury saw it for what it was—and acquitted me on that one too! The 'mistake' with the calibre at Innisfail had been intentional; the beginning of the pressure 'they' thought would break my will. I never did buckle and that is why the offences grew to 23.

Surrounding the indictable offences were another eight or so charges: three of them were *Nolo contendere* (under challenge it was established that the crimes had not even occurred!). Five were *Nolle prosequi* (the Crown lacked sufficient evidence to prosecute the offence).

Another providential feature in my case was that two more detectives swore on oath that they too had interviewed me over the same three-day period I was held at Innisfail. Obviously they hadn't compared notebooks because later during the trial, it was shown that Pinko and Railer's rendition had an unusual 'from memory' collocation weaved through all the answers in three 'confessions' allegedly made by me during those same three days. Yet throughout that same time period, the other interviewing detectives never alleged that I ever used the 'from memory' collocation in anything they allegedly recorded contemporaneously as coming from me!

During the Evidence in Chief at my trial, John J. finished his cross-examination of Pinko by asking one final question: "Do you have a speech pattern or word choice you use often?"

Pinko replied, "None, from memory."

I must now add that just prior to that question, John and I had counted thirteen 'from memory' uses by Pinko dur-

▲ Joe, 1986

ing fifteen minutes of cross-examination evidence. It's all on record in the Queensland High Court archives.

The remaining five counts were based on actual evidence, evidence that regrettably got me convicted—six years in a Queensland prison. It's something I wouldn't wish on anyone—except a corrupt cop!

Terry Lewis (the 1980 Commissioner of Queensland police) was one of the 86 witnesses who gave evidence against me at my trial. And he later received twelve years in prison for his crimes.

Release celebrations 1986 – ▲ Dawn & Joe ▼ Fritz & Joe

VERBAL

SPEECH SOWS—SILENCE REAPS

Verbal is a legal ploy
used to clinch a case.
The prosecutor must enjoy
mens-rea needs its grace.

By fabrication they create
a fate much worse than guilt.
You rot away in slow decay
bereft of all life's built.

Unlike Odysseus (the Greek)
who changed his human form,
these Calibans are human shaped
And wear a uniform.

Joe Tog

ADDENDUM

Fritz: Escaped from East Berlin (while the Berlin Wall was being built by the Russians to encircle that part of the Berlin population) to West Berlin where he was held as a juvenile Displaced Person. He later immigrated to South Australia. He was a total contradiction in terms: a good friend, loyal, truthful, and a person who could be trusted with your children. But if he didn't know you your property was at risk!

TELEX: an electronic piece of office equipment, not unlike a modern fax machine.

A few years later, I learned from Bruce why the internal screw never made it to my cell-door when the bars were being cut: a prisoner in his section had suddenly taken ill and required immediate attention!

The big guy who broke into Yatala Prison organised my escape.

The man who cut the bars in this story returned to Yugoslavia: he was killed fighting for his ethnic group's freedom and independence.

An actual escape-from-prison had less punishment consequences than if you were caught attempting-to-escape: once free, your case became public and therefore dealt with according to law, in most cases. But if caught in an attempt it was kept in-house where each prison dealt with it differently based on the type of prisoner held. A beating often came first, followed by a month or two in solitary confinement – or forced labour – and of course the mandatory loss of all remissions earned up till then if you were a sentenced prisoner. And after all that, a kangaroo-court was convened (Prison Governor's hearing) where you usually lost months of future remissions. Real deterrents existed to discourage escape – but once committed, real incentives existed to complete the escape!

Prison rule in the 70's was rigorous. For example, to be moved from one cell to another (a security practise used regularly) was easily done with two medium sized cardboard boxes holding everything allowed to be kept by an inmate in their cell: and a search of your cell whenever the whim caught them – day or night. Visits by family or friends were permitted once a month and outgoing letters were one per week and censored. All regulations had to be strictly adhered to – or else.

Music was piped in from a radio in the prison office and quite often carelessly tuned in. And mind games were played out every day!

Anything written for a legal defence (alibi etc.) had to be sown with deception and dead-ends because the police were often informed and even the prosecution. I became so adept at weaving misleading 'facts' into my court papers while on remand, that the Crown failed on a number of prosecutions against me because of that practice.

South Channel Fort is a man-made Island built as part of the coastal defence of Melbourne in the 1860's, situated in the southern end of Port Phillip Bay just off the coast of Sorrento. I was employed as Caretaker and Guide for twelve months by the Friends of the Fort (I lived underground in a network of rooms and tunnels) with a tug-boat provided as transport. The Fort was my first place of employment in Victoria after my return from South Australia where I had lived for eighteen months under the umbrella of a court-order against extradition to Victoria for an undischarged parole.

In 1988 I negotiated my voluntary return to Victoria to serve six months in a prison at Morwell River. When released, the only employment I could find was the Fort and that period working on the Island, being surrounded by ocean, people and storms, plus the kindness shown by the Friends reinforced daily my resolve to let go the past and move on.

Joe, 1998

More great titles in the Brolga true crime series

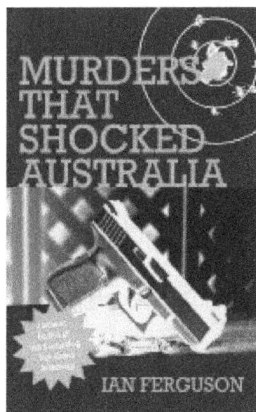

MurdersthatshockedAustralia
ISBN 9781921221538 $24.95

The second edition of this best-seller takes the reader through Australia's most challenging murders and personalities, from Ned Kelly to the baffling Pyjama Girl case. Enthralling and chilling, Ian Ferguson explores the true-life cases that have gripped Australia and our media.

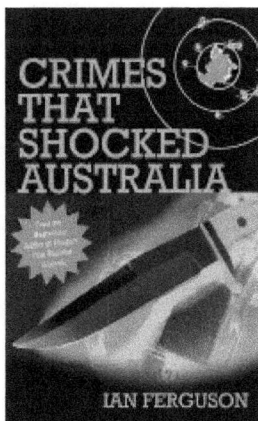

CrimesthatshockedAustralia
ISBN 9781921221569 $24.95

A true crime anthology of shocking proportions. With enough gruesome tales to send shivers up your spine, including gangland muders, kidnappings, hold-ups, mutilation and more. These crimes that occurred in our own backyard are hard to believe and not easy to forget.

For order details see next page.

Fill in the form below to order one or more of these great titles

		Qty
Aussie Prison Breaks by Joe Tog	AU$24.95	.....
Murders that shocked Australia by Ian Ferguson	AU$24.95	.....
Crimes that shocked Australia by Ian Ferguson	AU$24.95	.....
Postage within Australia	AU $5.00	.....

TOTAL★ $_____

★ All prices include GST

Name: ....

Address: ....

Phone: ....

Email Address: ....

Payment: ❑ Money Order ❑ Cheque ❑ Amex ❑ MasterCard ❑ Visa

Cardholder's Name: ....

Credit Card Number: ....

Signature: ....

Expiry Date: ....

Allow 7 days for delivery.

Payment to: Better Bookshop (ABN 14 067 257 390)
               PO Box 12544
               A'Beckett Street, Melbourne, 8006
               Victoria, Australia
               Fax: +61 3 9671 4730
               admin@brolgapublishing.com.au

BE PUBLISHED

Publishing through a successful Australian publisher.
Brolga provides:
- Editorial appraisal
- Cover design
- Typesetting
- Printing
- Author promotion
- National book trade distribution, including
sales, marketing and distribution through
Macmillan Australia.
- International book trade distribution
- World-wide e-Book distribution

For details and inquiries, contact:
Brolga Publishing Pty Ltd
PO Box 12544
A'Beckett St VIC 8006

Phone: 0414 608 494
admin@brolgapublishing.com.au
markzocchi@brolgapublishing.com.au

ABN: 46 063 962 443

www.ingramcontent.com/pod-product-compliance
Lightning Source LLC
Chambersburg PA
CBHW071432090426
42737CB00011B/1635